The
RUSSIANS
and
REAGAN

The RUSSIANS *and* REAGAN

Strobe Talbott

Foreword by Cyrus R. Vance

A Council on Foreign Relations Book

Vintage Books • A Division of Random House • New York

Council on Foreign Relations Books

The Council on Foreign Relations, Inc., is a nonprofit and nonpartisan organization devoted to promoting improved understanding of international affairs through the free exchange of ideas. The Council does not take any position on questions of foreign policy and has no affiliation with, and receives no funding from, the United States government.

From time to time, books and monographs written by members of the Council's research staff or visiting fellows, or commissioned by the Council, or written by an independent author with critical review contributed by a Council study or working group are published with the designation "Council on Foreign Relations Book." Any book or monograph bearing that designation is, in the judgment of the Committee on Studies of the Council's board of directors, a responsible treatment of a significant international topic worthy of presentation to the public. All statements of fact and expressions of opinion contained in Council books are, however, the sole responsibility of the author.

A Vintage Original, March 1984
First Edition

Copyright © 1984 by The Council on Foreign Relations, Inc. All rights reserved under International and Pan-American Copyright Conventions. Published in the United States by Random House, Inc., New York, and simultaneously in Canada by Random House of Canada Limited, Toronto.

Library of Congress Cataloging in Publication Data
Talbott, Strobe. The Russians and Reagan.
"A Council on Foreign Relations book."
1. United States—Foreign relations—Soviet Union.
2. Soviet Union—Foreign relations—United States.
3. Reagan, Ronald.
4. United States—Foreign relations—1981–   .
5. Soviet Union—Foreign relations—1975–   .
I. Title.
E183.8.S65T35   1984   327.73047   84-40076
ISBN 0-394-72635-9 (pbk.)

Manufactured in the United States of America

To my teachers:
Clinton Ely,
Vadim Liapunov,
and, in memory,
Max Hayward

CONTENTS

FOREWORD
Cyrus R. Vance

In this nuclear age, the relationship between the Soviet Union and the United States is critically important, affecting not only the daily lives of American and Soviet citizens, but also the lives of peoples around the globe. The ultimate fate of our relations with Moscow shadows the very future of our planet.

Our volatile relationship with Russia has periodically swung between euphoria and dark pessimism. Today, relations are close to an all-time low, especially insofar as communications between our two capitals are concerned. In these turbulent times, if we are to act wisely in dealing with the Soviet Union, it is essential that we understand how we have come to this low point and what this state of affairs portends for the future.

No one is better equipped to provide such an analysis than Strobe Talbott, who brings to the task a broad understanding of the U.S.S.R. and East-West relations. Translator-editor of two volumes of Nikita Khrushchev's memoirs, author of *Endgame: The Inside Story of SALT II* (the best work that has been done on the SALT II negotiations) and of *Deadly Gambits,* a forthcoming book on the recent strategic and intermediate-range nuclear weapons talks, Mr. Talbott is a much admired and highly respected journalist. As diplomatic correspondent of *Time*, he has developed a profound knowledge of the Soviet system through long study and extensive contact with Soviet party officials, journalists, diplomats, and experts attached to the foreign policy institutes in Moscow. I have known Mr. Talbott for many years both as a friend and as a skilled and discerning reporter, and I have the highest regard for his work.

This is a fascinating and important book about Soviet perceptions of the Reagan Administration. Neglect of this topic can lead to misunderstandings on both sides which, in times of high tension, are especially dangerous.

While I believe it unlikely that either nation would deliberately initiate a pre-emptive nuclear strike against the other, it is possible that, by accident or miscalculation, we could stumble into a nuclear conflict, particularly in such regions as the Middle East and Southwest Asia. If we are to reduce this risk of miscalculation and make progress in re-establishing a serious dialogue on controlling nuclear weapons, as we must, it is imperative that we understand our interlocutors, their motivation, and their perception of our words and actions. Since the Soviet Union is a powerful country with values that are very different from ours, we are caught up in a continuing ideological struggle that is unlikely to abate in the foreseeable future. This does not mean, however, that it is beyond our power to find a way to live together in this imperfect world and to develop a working relationship to lessen the chance of military conflict between us—a conflict that could destroy us both. Most of us would agree that there can be no victor in a nuclear war and that the two superpowers—and all other countries—are in the same boat and will survive or founder together.

There is, I believe, one overriding truth in the aftermath of Hiroshima—no nation can achieve true security by itself. No matter how many weapons a nation develops, no matter how strong its armed forces become, they can never guarantee freedom from attack. Both the United States and the Soviet Union are, and will remain, vulnerable to nuclear attack. To guarantee our own security we must face this reality and work with other nations, including the Soviet Union, to achieve common security. For security in the nuclear age means *common* security. On this issue there should be no division between left and right.

In leading us through a thought provoking and informed analysis of the public statements and actions of U.S. and Soviet leaders, Mr. Talbott illuminates the developing perceptions of both sides over the past three years. It is an engrossing and disquieting tale told with skill, fairness, and insight.

Mr. Talbott concludes there is reason to believe that at the end of last year the Soviet leadership had been persuaded, "finally," by the rhetoric and actions of the Reagan Administration that the United States was bent on destruction of the Soviet form of government, and that the objective of the Reagan Administration in the arms control negotiations was "to turn back the clock on military parity and regain for the United States the superiority it had enjoyed before the era of détente."

What these Soviet perceptions may hold for the future remains to be seen. Certainly the following statement of the late President Andropov in his September 28, 1983, pronouncement has a baleful ring: "Even if someone had any illusions about the possible evolution for the better in the policy of the present U.S. Administration, the latest developments have finally dispelled them."

As Mr. Talbott points out, we do not know whether the Andropov statement is a strategic or tactical move.

If it is the former, we will face a long period of confrontation; if it is the latter, some flexibility in the Soviet position may develop in the months ahead, as the Reagan Administration seeks to deal with Andropov's successor, Konstantin Chernenko. In my judgment it is most likely, as Mr. Talbott suggests, that the unyielding Soviet position will hold for the next year. This means that not only is there little likelihood that any serious business will be done between the Soviet Union and the United States until our elections are over, but also the months immediately ahead will be marked by tension and danger.

Cyrus R. Vance
New York, February 13, 1984

PREFACE

This book grew out of my participation in a Council on Foreign Relations study group on the Soviet Union and the Reagan Administration, which met five times during the spring of 1983. I am grateful to the other participants in that group and to its chairman, Henry Grunwald, as well as to those who offered helpful suggestions at an additional meeting organized by the Council to review my manuscript in November 1983.

Neither the study group nor the review session was intended to produce a consensus. Rather, the object of the exercise was what in Soviet jargon is known as "a frank and comradely exchange of views"—an intelligent discussion among people with differing backgrounds and perspectives, hence often with sharply differing opinions about the complicated subject at hand. Therefore in no sense have I tried to speak for my fellow participants, nor am I under any illusion that all, or even most, of them share my own views.

I am particularly grateful to Robert Legvold, the director of the study group, and Susan Pederson, the rapporteur; Michael Mandelbaum of the Lehrman Institute, for sharing with me his own synthesis of the group's proceedings and analysis of the issues; and, for their encouragement and editorial guidance, David Kellogg, the Council's Publications Director, Paul Kreisberg, its Director of Studies, and Jason Epstein of Random House.

Some of the thoughts developed here came into focus during my reporting and writing assignments for *Time*. My colleagues there, particularly Ray Cave and Richard Duncan, have been extremely supportive of my work, even when it has carried me afield from weekly journalism. To them also, my thanks.

S.T.   *February 13, 1984*

The
RUSSIANS
and
REAGAN

THE DEBATE ON
THE HOME FRONT

During 1983, the tone and substance of Soviet-American relations went from bad at the beginning of the year, to relatively and very tentatively better during the summer, to suddenly much worse in the fall, to absolutely awful at the end—the worst in more than two decades.

As so often in the past, the much-maligned and star-crossed enterprise of arms control had to bear the brunt of adverse developments. It had become fashionable on the American side to complain that the superpowers' negotiation of agreements on the composition and deployment of their nuclear arsenals was grossly overrated as a mechanism for regulating their competition. For all their differences, many liberals, moderates and conservatives seemed to share disillusionment with the arms-control process.

Whether that disillusionment was well founded or not, it was, in a way, beside the point. Regardless of whether arms control had been invested with too much hope back in the days of détente, or burdened with too much blame in the days since, the fact remained that arms control had been—and still was—a touchstone of the relationship, if only because there was so little engagement on other issues. Whatever the broader agenda between the superpowers *ought* to be, arms control has been, for all intents and purposes, one of the few items of active business to have survived the tribulations of recent years. Yet by December 1983, engagement there, too, had ended, at least temporarily, for the first time in fourteen years. The U.S.S.R. suspended its participation in all three sets of arms-control negotiations with the United States: the two on strategic and intermediate-range nuclear weapons in Geneva and the third on conventional forces in Vienna.

The Reagan Administration was concerned about the walkouts, the break-offs, and the appearance of an overall breakdown in East-West relations. There was nervousness both in the alliance and at home about whether the tensions were likely to get out of control. To allay those fears, the Administration adopted an optimistic line about the near future. Having come into office crying, "The Russians are coming!" the Administration ended its third year with the soothing prediction that "the Russians will be back" at the bargaining tables in Geneva and Vienna. Not only did U.S. officials foresee a turnaround in 1984—they offered to help bring it about by having Secretary of State George Shultz go to Stockholm for the 35-nation Conference on Disarmament in Europe with the announced hope of talking to his Soviet counterpart, Andrei Gromyko, early in the new year.

On January 16, President Reagan delivered a speech on the need for "peaceful competition" and on the superpowers' "common interest" in avoiding war and reducing the level of arms.* America's West European allies were quick to welcome the tone of the speech, but the Soviets were just as quick to note the absence of any change in the substance of U.S. policy (such as new proposals for the deadlocked arms negotiations) and to dismiss Reagan's somewhat softer words as a cynical, election-year maneuver.

*For the text of this and other major speeches, see Appendices.

Shultz's mission to Stockholm was undertaken largely to satisfy the desire of West Europeans, Congress and the American public to see U.S. and Soviet officials shaking hands and talking again after the spectacle of the walkouts in 1983. Gromyko was coy about whether he would go to Stockholm at all. When he did go, it was for one of the same reasons as Shultz: to please the West European gallery with his appearance (though not, as turned out, with his words).

For many of Shultz's colleagues in Washington and Gromyko's in Moscow, diplomacy had become more than ever an exercise in public relations and the Soviet-American dialogue an exercise in propaganda. What mattered more than the Foreign Minister's travels was that the Kremlin was laying the ground for military activities and political conditions that would make difficult the resumption of the arms-control talks, to say nothing of progress toward an agreement.

At the same time that Shultz was preparing to go to Stockholm, the White House was putting the finishing touches on a bill of particulars in support of its long-standing accusation that the U.S.S.R. had violated virtually all the arms-control agreements to which it was party. That report went to Congress at the end of January, and it partially undercut the effect of the President's relatively mild speech and the Shultz-Gromyko handshake of the week before.

Nor did what transpired between Shultz and Gromyko in Stockholm seem to turn over a new leaf in the relationship. In his address to the conference, Shultz chastised the U.S.S.R. for having erected an "artificial barrier" in Europe that "cruelly divided this continent—and, indeed, heartlessly divided one of its great nations [Germany]." While Shultz's speech sounded some sour notes, Gromyko's spewed vitriol. He railed against the United States for its "maniacal plans," "criminal and dishonest methods," and "pathological obsession" with rearmament. He dismissed the Reagan speech of a few days before as a "hackneyed ploy" that deceived no one: "It is deeds that are needed, not verbal exercises."

Shultz and Gromyko also met for five hours in private. The exchange was described as "intense" and "businesslike." It produced indications that the negotiations on conventional-arms reductions might be resumed in Vienna and that a new round of quiet diplomacy might take place in Washington and Moscow toward a resumption of nuclear-arms negotiations as well, but the two sides remained at loggerheads on the issues involved in the Strategic Arms Reduction Talks (START) and Intermediate-range Nuclear Forces (INF) talks.

On January 24, *Pravda* published what it described as an interview with the top Soviet leader, Yuri Andropov, who had not been seen in public in over five months and was suffering from a serious kidney ailment. Andropov's statements were not quite as harsh as Gromyko's, but they were hardly conciliatory. He attacked the United States for "torpedoing" the arms talks and "perpetrating imperialist brigandage" around the world. He expressed skepticism about whether Reagan's speech the week before signaled any change in the substance of U.S. policy; and while he held open the possibility of resuming negotiations, he made clear that it would have to be on Soviet terms.

In a private letter to Reagan, Andropov reiterated that an improvement in relations would depend on a significant shift in American policy. It was the last communication between them. On February 9, Andropov died, plunging the Soviet Union into a period of leadership transition that would coincide with an American presidential election campaign.

Thus, the auguries for the new year were as inauspicious as the record of the old was dismal. On this, there was little debate in the United States. There was, however, considerable debate on a range of other questions, and that debate continues.

Is world peace necessarily any more in peril with the relationship between the superpowers at a twenty-year low? President Reagan said no. He insisted that those who saw "an increased danger of conflict" were "profoundly mistaken." He and defenders of Administration policy believed that the Soviet leaders would be far less likely to risk direct armed conflict with the United States—or stumble into Third World misadventures that might lead to such conflict—when opposed by an American leadership that has proved itself to be vigilant, self-confident, and committed both to remaining strong and, when and where necessary, using force.

Others worried that it was the President who was profoundly mistaken and that his policies had forced the Soviets into a corner from which they might yet lash out in some unpredictable way so as, in the words of one commentator, "to reassert their international status and teach Reagan a lesson."*

*This was the warning of Seweryn Bialer, an expert on the U.S.S.R. at Columbia University, in an article in *The Washington Post* (January 22, 1984) shortly after his return from a visit to Moscow: "I found combative, angry people in the Soviet capital. Among the members of the political elite feelings verge on rage, and there is a mood of defiance." Bialer expanded on his ominous view in "Danger in Moscow," in *The New York Review of Books* (February 16, 1984).

Andropov himself, in his January 24, 1984, reply to Reagan, had described the situation as "acute and dangerous," adding, "It is impermissible to display an underestimation of it."

Whether the risk of war was underestimated by the Administration or exaggerated and exploited by the Kremlin, there was, at the beginning of 1984, certainly a heightened sense of danger both in the United States and in Europe. This the public opinion polls at home and cautionary, anxious, sometimes almost pleading comments from across the Atlantic made clear. For that reason, the deterioration in the superpower relationship was almost certain to have consequences in the American domestic political arena, including in the presidential elections, as well as in the politics of the Western alliance.

What those consequences would be was difficult to anticipate, particularly on the home front. President Reagan's Democratic challengers, notably the front-runner Walter Mondale, were sure to make the most of foreign-policy issues in the campaign. With different emphasis and somewhat different prescriptions, they were, early in 1984, all accusing the Administration of being too confrontational and of letting opportunities for constructive diplomacy slip away.

The Democrats were trying to put Reagan on the defensive with a variation on a theme that he had used to devastating effect against Jimmy Carter in 1980. During his television debate with Carter, Reagan had asked the American electorate if it was better off than four years before. The question clearly referred to economic well-being; it resonated with the national discontent over inflation and recession; it invited—and, at the polls in November 1980, received—a negative answer.

Now the Democrats were asking whether the American electorate felt *safer* after four years of Reagan than before. This time the question was meant to resonate with the national unease, reflected in public opinion surveys and in Congress, over the deepening American military involvement in the Middle East and Central America, and also over the Soviet-American stand-off.

The Democrats, however, could not be sure whether the Soviet factor in the foreign-policy issue would, come November, cut in their favor or redound to the benefit of the President himself. Patriotism, anti-Communism, and mistrust of the Soviet Union and all its works run at least as deep in the United States as the desire for arms control and the eagerness to applaud presidential statesmanship and summitry. The American people want their President to stand up to the Soviets in the political, military and ideological rivalry between the superpowers just as much as they want him to sit down with them at the conference table.

Reagan's defense of his record depended largely on his claim that he had succeeded dramatically in standing up to the Soviets with his hard line and his military buildup; that he had indeed made the world safer by doing so, for the Soviets, despite their anger, were respectful of a tougher American leadership and deterred by it; and, moreover, that he had demonstrated his willingness to sit down with them as well. It was they who had walked away from the table. By professing confidence that they would come back, he was seeking to keep the onus on them for having walked out in the first place. The broader implication was that the Soviets were responsible for the breakdown in relations more generally.

...ultz and Gromyko devoted much of their rhetoric ...tockholm to assigning each other virtually 100 percent of the blame for what had come widely to be seen as a new Cold War. The Reagan Administration had a considerable stake in convincing American voters and allies that Shultz was right and Gromyko was wrong; the Administration had to fend off the charge that the United States bore some responsibility for the sorry state of relations—a charge that had been made not just by the Soviets, but by the Administration's American and West European critics.

Underlying this part of the debate was another issue: how to interpret the Soviet side of the story—indeed, whether to listen to it at all. Defenders of current U.S. policy tend to dismiss Soviet complaints as deliberately misleading and to recommend that policymakers pay those complaints little heed, lest the United States be distracted from staying the course that the Administration has set.

But for those who believe that the Reagan Administration has unwisely exacerbated Soviet-American relations, Soviet complaints are more worthy of attention—skeptical attention, to be sure, but not dismissal. One need not accept the Soviet side of the story to derive from it some insight into the motivation and mentality of the rulers with whom the United States is trying to deal, some lessons about the future, and some hope that the the next chapter in the story will not be as melancholy as the one which ended in December 1983.

THE PERCEPTION PERPLEX

This book is about perceptions—how the leaders of another nation, the U.S.S.R., see the leaders of our own nation. It is based largely on my encounters over the last three years with that cadre of journalists, Party officials, diplomats and *institutchiki* (experts attached to the foreign-policy institutes in Moscow) whom the Soviet regime has authorized to serve as professional purveyors of Soviet perceptions of the United States.* Both the subject and the sources of this book are controversial in themselves and require some preliminary discussion.

A corollary to the old adage, "Know thine enemy," ought to be, "Know how he knows you"—particularly when the adversary is the Soviet Union, whose behavior is often reactive. How the Soviet leaders react and what they are likely to do next are questions better

*There have been numerous published writings on the various aspects of the subject, including a useful article, "Reagan Through Soviet Eyes," in the autumn 1983 issue of *Foreign Policy* by two members of the Council on Foreign Relations study group, its director, Robert Legvold, and Lawrence Caldwell. Also see "Reagan and Russia," by Seweryn Bialer and Joan Afferica, in the winter 1982/83 issue of *Foreign Affairs*; and *Soviet Perceptions of the United States* by Morton Schwartz, also a member of the study group (University of California Press, 1978). I have made use in the pages that follow of citations from some of the discussion papers prepared for the study group as well as comments offered by group members at the review session in November.

answered if we have a clear sense of why they think we have done something and what they think we will do next.

This is why the words "perception" and "misperception" are commonplace in discussions of Soviet-American relations, even though some experts and policymakers consider the views of Soviet leaders unknowable by definition, hidden away in the most inaccessible corner of the black box of the Soviet political system. Others see an American interest in Soviet perceptions as a symptom of softheadedness: trying to understand how the Soviets see the world may lead an American analyst onto a slippery slope; he will end up giving the Soviets the benefit of doubts they do not deserve and accepting at face value their self-serving, disingenuous rationale for the way they behave in the world.

The Soviets are in fact extremely secretive, though in manipulative and deceitful ways they can also be highly communicative. In a sense, we have less than nothing to go on. Not only do the Soviets do their best, which is very good indeed, to keep us from knowing what they are really thinking, but they also do all they can, which is a lot, to make us think that they are thinking what they want us to think they are thinking, as opposed to what they are really thinking. In particular, they want us to think that they are firm and realistic, that they take the long view; that they understand how we operate and are patient but principled in dealing with us. They adopt the posture of a strict but long-suffering adult who is coping with a moody, petulant adolescent. Sometimes they want us to think they are on the brink of losing patience, that our leaders have pushed them too far.

They have built up an entire apparatus that seeks to manipulate our perceptions of their perceptions of us. This apparatus has multiple centers: the Soviet press, the foreign-policy institutes, the Ministry of Foreign Affairs, the International Information Department of the Central Committee, and, without doubt, the KGB. Some American experts believe that the *institutchiki* themselves are little more than the front men for the disinformation department of the KGB, and that their principal purpose is to play upon American hopes when relations are good and fears when they are bad.

Be that as it may, there is no question that one of the many frustrations of being on the American end of the dialogue with representatives of that apparatus is the near impossibility of getting them to acknowledge that their government bears some responsibility for the deterioration in the relationship. At conference after conference, the dreary pattern is the same. American participants, particularly those inclined toward liberal views, try to break the ice with speeches about how relations are in a sorry state and both sides are to blame. The Soviet participants reply, in effect and often in so many words, "Well, you're half right: your side is to blame."

Once, during an afternoon-long session at the Institute for the Study of the U.S.A. and Canada in Moscow, I felt I had fulfilled my quota of candor about American responsibility and that my hosts had been too quick to amplify my remarks with further denunciations of the United States.

"All right," I said, "let's see if any one of you can name so much as a single thing that your side may have done wrong in the past seven years that has contributed to the problem."

There was a long, awkward pause. Finally one of the Soviets spoke up: "To be frank, our side probably has made a mistake in underestimating the capacity of the United States to shift course erratically and to plunge into periods of hysteria. Or to put it differently, we overestimated the stability and the continuity of the American political system."

"Thanks a lot," I said, suddenly weary of my travels.

At a dinner in Washington on November 16, 1983, to commemorate the fiftieth anniversary of the establishment of diplomatic relations between the United States and the Soviet Union, Anatoly Dobrynin, the longtime Soviet ambassador to the United States, listened patiently to a barrage of criticism from various Americans, then remarked, "I did not come here to say we're all right, and you're all wrong." It was graciously and diplomatically put; but regardless of what he had come to say, he had certainly not come to *deny* that his side was all right and the United States was all wrong.

On top of the blatant, sometimes infuriating one-sidedness of what passes for analysis in the U.S.S.R., there is reason to question both the quality of Soviet expertise about the United States and the extent to which the experts' advice penetrates to the core of the policymaking process. If their society is a black box to us, ours is a hall of mirrors to them. Much is made of the bonanza that our open press offers them. No doubt all that information helps them immensely in gathering military and technological intelligence, but what about the more important task of synthesizing a coherent, comprehensive and realistic view of how America works? The Soviets have an extraordinary penchant for misapplying the conspiratorial norms that govern their political process in their attempts at understanding ours. A dramatic example is the persistent suspicion, entertained by Soviets who should know better, that Watergate was a plot perpetrated against Richard Nixon by the enemies of détente, or, alternatively, that Nixon was abandoned by the "ruling circles" of the Eastern Establishment when he encountered difficulties.

Once one has gotten over being dazzled by their idiomatic American English, one often finds that Soviet experts on the United States suffer from compartmentalization and overspecialization. An *institutchik* may know a great deal about congressional elections or the anti-Vietnam protest movement of the 1960s or the relationship between the executive and legislative branches of the U.S. government or the evolution of the American cruise missile program, but it is rare to encounter Soviets with a sound, comprehensive understanding of the dynamics of American politics and society.

These impediments to dialogue with Soviet spokesmen—their refusal to engage in genuine, open-minded analysis of the origins of the current state of affairs, and their shortcomings as interpreters of our system—reinforce skepticism about whether they are good sources for an understanding of how their leadership reacts to ours.

But this skepticism can be misplaced and overdrawn. To be sure, there is a danger of relying too much on the few chosen representatives of the official view. But there is also a danger of relying too little—of discounting virtually anything they say as disinformation. More particularly, there is a danger of not attending to their attempts at explaining the psychological or emotional factors at work in the Kremlin. When they talk about wounded pride or anger or frustration or disappointment or fear on the part of Politburo members, there is a tendency to dismiss it as a cynical Soviet attempt to exploit the well-known American capacity for self-criticism. Either that, or American experts often suspect that what they are really hearing is Soviet *détenteniks* fretting about their own careers and transferring their anxieties to their invisible superiors.

Some American experts, particularly those who support Administration policies, go so far as to suggest that critics of those policies are hearing what they want to hear from Soviet spokesmen and promulgating their own criticisms under the guise of "Soviet perceptions"; that American *détenteniks* are transferring their own point of view to their Soviet interlocutors. A more extreme version of this charge—one that comes close to red-baiting—is that anyone who takes Soviet complaints seriously, as anything other than Orwellian chicanery, is aiding and abetting the Soviet cause.

There is, in the United States, a widespread predisposition to believe that for all their huffing and puffing, the Soviets will, when the chips are down, coolly calculate where their interests lie and then march purposefully in that direction. According to this view, when a Soviet leader wrings his hands or shakes his fist, he is responding in kind to harsh American rhetoric or engaging in psychological warfare; he is not, however, necessarily indicating what his government will actually *do*.

Other experts look at Soviet behavior in terms of bureaucratic politics: various leaders represent certain parochial interests, and act according to the requirements of their organizations. The military wants more weapons; the diplomats want more agreements. When diplomacy seems to have reached a dead end, the military wields more influence in the councils of power. Those who hold this view of the Russians tend to be more pessimistic about the current situation than those who impute an overarching rationality to the Soviet system.

Still others argue, rather forlornly of late, for paying attention to factors that are neither bureaucratic nor entirely rational—anger, pride, and fear. Such human factors are as important to understanding what the United States is up against as the disposition and capability of weapons. Arguably, human factors are more important, since the wrong combination of such factors could, *in extremis*, cause the weapons to go off. One of America's most experienced students of the Soviet Union, George Kennan, has warned repeatedly that anti-Sovietism has led to the "dehumanization" of the Soviet leaders in American eyes. There has been a natural accompanying tendency in American analysis to dismiss the human factors in Soviet behavior.

Probably something like this has happened to the Soviet view of American behavior as well. It would be a pity if, as a result of the recent deterioration in Soviet-American relations, those who have a stake in worst-case analysis of what the enemy is and what he is likely to do next were to prevail on both sides.

It is easy enough to debate and discredit the Soviet Union's America-watchers in what they have to say about us. But that is not at issue here. What is at issue is what the Russians have to tell us about how their leaders are reacting to our leaders. On that score, our own experts have not done so well either. The American assumption has been mainly that the Soviet leaders probably see the Reagan Administration much as the

Administration sees itself: tough but reasonable, with a bark considerably worse than its bite.

It took Yuri Andropov himself to offer the most authoritative challenge to that view.

TALKING TOUGH AND WALKING OUT

Andropov came to the pinnacle of power in November 1982 and headed straight for the podium, announcing a campaign to restore economic efficiency and social discipline. Then, barely catching his breath, he delivered a long sequence of full-dress foreign-policy speeches, "interviews" with *Pravda*, and stroking sessions with visiting Westerners in which he advanced a series of arms-control proposals, coupled with threats. These were intended to advance the Soviet objective of stopping the deployment of American missiles in Western Europe.

Andropov failed to make much of a dent in the sluggish system at home or to forestall the deployment of new weapons abroad, and he did not live up to his early billing as a new, more modern, more sophisticated, more Western-style Soviet leader—except in one respect: more than any previous General Secretary he obviously believed in the power of words and regarded his speeches and other statements not simply as explanations of policy, but as ways of implementing that policy. But as effective as his delivery was, his follow-through was less impressive. In this regard, Andropov was like Ronald Reagan. Both men put great stock in speeches and public statements—not, however, to communicate with each other, but to trade accusations and denunciations. Andropov and Reagan were both inclined to play to public opinion, particularly on those issues where Soviet-American relations have been most contentious.

The name-calling reached its peak after the Soviets shot down a Korean airliner on August 31, 1983. First George Shultz, then Reagan himself condemned the outrage in the harshest terms, in effect calling the U.S.S.R. an international outlaw. As though to underscore this accusation, American authorities then prevented Gromyko from landing at a New York airport, forcing him to cancel his appearance at the United Nations General Assembly.

The circumstances of the airliner incident were less clear-cut than the American response at first made them seem. The United States assumed that the Soviets had positively identified the plane as a civilian airliner before they shot it down. Only later did it emerge that the Soviets believed they were intercepting a military spy plane. In its understandable horror over what the Soviets had done—but also in its haste to take advantage of what seemed an ideal propaganda opportunity—the Reagan Administration overplayed its hand. It accused the U.S.S.R. of committing premeditated mass murder when the correct charge was manslaughter and criminal negligence for failing to distinguish the plane as an airliner.

It was in this harsh atmosphere that Andropov on September 28, 1983, denounced President Reagan's management of the relationship between the superpowers.* In one respect, Andropov was answering Reagan, who had just delivered a speech of his own to the United Nations reiterating his condemnation of the Soviets for having shot down the Korean plane and adjusting the U.S. negotiating position in the European nuclear arms-control talks not so much to make the American proposal more palatable to the Soviet Union as to make deployment more palatable to the West Europeans.

But Andropov's statement was much more than just another outburst in the shouting match that the two leaderships had been waging for three years. Andropov's statement had the ring of a last word, not a defense against Reagan's latest charges but a prosecutor's summing-up; Andropov was seeking to convict the United States for killing détente. It was a polemical *tour de force*, the most comprehensive, categorical denunciation of a U.S. Administration by a top Soviet leader since the darkest, coldest days of the Cold War.

Andropov's denunciation was obviously drafted with great care, the product of long sessions involving many members of the collective leadership. It was thus more significant than Nikita Khrushchev's rantings at the United Nations or in Paris during the U-2 affair in 1960. Andropov's statement seemed to be a formal declaration of what the Politburo as a whole wanted the world—and perhaps more important, the Soviet people—to think was its assessment of the Reagan Administration.

That assessment could hardly have been bleaker, not only in its list of past grievances, but in its prognosis. Andropov came within a hair of stating flatly that he

*See Appendix.

and the men for whom he was speaking wanted nothing more to do with the Reagan Administration.

Thus the statement was certainly the most authoritative and explicit answer so far to a question that had been causing intense debate in Washington and elsewhere for the past three years: how does the Soviet leadership perceive the Reagan Administration, and, hence, what does this perception bode for the future?

The Reagan Administration had its own, rather sanguine answer to that question. Naturally the Kremlin was not happy to see the U.S. government in the hands of the most uncompromisingly anti-Soviet Administration since World War II, but the Kremlin leaders are pragmatic enough to recognize that Ronald Reagan is the only U.S. President they've got to deal with—and therefore, quite simply, they've got to deal with him. Also, they are prudent enough to take Reagan's tough stance seriously, and to be restrained by it. In short, hardliners in Moscow may not like hardliners in Washington, but they respect them, and are deterred by them.

In practice, this official American attitude meant a persistent confidence, even smugness, about the prospects for an arms-control agreement and a summit meeting in 1984, when Reagan would most need them to outflank the Democrats on the war-and-peace issue. The Administration assumed that the Soviets must have known they could get a better deal from Ronald Reagan before the 1984 election, when he would be under political pressure to demonstrate his statesmanship.

There was considerable talk about "the 1972 precedent." This referred to Richard Nixon's ability to have a summit meeting with Brezhnev and sign the

SALT I agreements in May 1972—just after he had bombed the Soviet Union's ally, North Vietnam, and shortly before he faced a liberal Democrat, George McGovern, in a presidential election.

The analogy between 1972 and 1984 was, to put it mildly, overdrawn. Whatever the superficial similarities, there were important differences. The biggest was that by 1972, Nixon and Brezhnev had already established détente; they had a working, productive, promising relationship, durable enough to withstand the bombing of North Vietnam; Nixon was, almost certainly, the Soviets' choice to win the election. The relationship between the Reagan Administration and the Kremlin in 1984 could hardly have been in sharper contrast.

On the eve of the Andropov statement of September 28, 1983, Administration officials expressed confidence that an upturn was inevitable and even imminent. The Soviets, according to this view, must be smart enough to see that behind the Administration's tough rhetoric was an increasingly moderate policy; the Soviets' self-interest would prevent them from slamming the door on the arms-control talks in Geneva after NATO deployment had begun. A walkout there would undercut their peace campaign in Western Europe, make them look like spoilers, and let the United States off the hook in the negotiations.

Then came Andropov's statement. His message could be paraphrased in a colloquialism made famous by one of his countrymen, a pilot attached to the Far Eastern Air Defense Command, a few weeks before. After listening to nearly three years of American conventional wisdom and wishful thinking about how the

Kremlin views the Reagan Administration, Andropov said, in effect, "Fiddlesticks!"

Some commentators, and some officials in the Reagan Administration, initially dismissed Andropov's blast as mere words. But they were words that he and his comrades would now have either to make good on or eat. They were not necessarily fighting words (although Kennan has pointed out repeatedly that in the age before nuclear weapons, invective of this sort would almost certainly be a prologue to war). Rather, Andropov's were giving-up words, picking-up-his-marbles-and-going-home words. And this is what the Soviets did by the end of the year when they walked out of the negotiations on Intermediate-range Nuclear Forces (INF) and refused to agree to dates for the resumption of the ones on strategic and conventional forces.

The Soviet leaders seemed to have made a decision about the nature of their American counterparts and how to deal with them. Contrary to the optimistic analysis favored by the Administration, the Soviets chose to overlook the evidence of ambivalence, moderation, traditionalism and restraint within the Administration; they chose to pay attention instead to those trends in American policy that seemed most menacing. It was with those signs squarely in focus, and all others at the periphery of their vision, that the Soviets apparently decided that this particular Administration's anti-Sovietism had an implacable and assertive quality, a real difference that required a more implacable and assertive Soviet response.

If this was indeed the Soviet reaction to Reagan, it had been a long time coming.

ANYBODY BUT CARTER

There is nothing new about Soviet leaders complaining about American policies. Vladimir Lenin and all his successors have charged the United States with being out to get the U.S.S.R., and they have used that accusation of unrelieved hostility to help justify their accumulation of military power, their subjugation of other countries, and their repression of their own people.

In the last decade or so, the Soviets added a new grievance to their long bill of particulars: in addition to being hostile, the U.S. was inconsistent, unpredictable, even unstable; it was constantly changing leaders and those leaders were constantly changing policies. The litany has been that the Soviet Union wants to deal with the United States as with any other nation, not "with this or that clique," a tiresome theme, especially insofar as it implies that Soviet foreign policy is exemplary.

This professed devotion to consistency serves a number of purposes, and reveals a number of things about the Soviet leadership itself. For all their revolutionary pretensions, the old men in the Kremlin are, ideology aside, profoundly conservative. They hate change; they hate unpredictability; they prefer the devil they know, yet they are constantly finding themselves confronted with ones they don't know in Washington. By congratulating themselves for their own "maturity" and remonstrating with the United States for its "childishness," they are trying to make a virtue out of their own

24

hidebound system. They seem deaf to the irony in their own words, given the literally extreme maturity of their leadership.

By the time Reagan came along, Soviet students of the United States seemed to have accepted vacillation and discontinuity as a permanent feature of the American system; and at the very beginning of the new Administration, some of them even ventured the opinion that there were certain consolations. For one thing, while the ever-confounding American political process could throw up an implausible President like Jimmy Carter, it could also throw him out. For another, American political figures seemed astonishingly quick to change their tune and their spots to suit new ambitions, circumstances and responsibilities. Ronald Reagan's background as a fire-breathing right-winger led them to expect that a change could only be for the better. A number of Soviets in late 1980 and early 1981 expressed cautious confidence that the very institution of the presidency was conducive to pragmatism; its effect on Reagan would be mellowing, or, another favorite word, "sobering." Reagan would be coaxed by his own countrymen toward the center.

The Soviets hadn't yet thought much about the possibility that the center itself had shifted dramatically to the right in American politics. In talking, with undisguised relief, about the departing Carter Administration, Soviet scholars noted that while Zbigniew Brzezinski, a detestable anti-Soviet in their view, may have won out, at least Cyrus Vance had been there for most of the Administration, representing centrism and pragmatism.

According to some accounts, the Soviet embassy in Washington had forecast that Carter would be re-elected, while the institutes in Moscow were betting on a Reagan victory. Yet both sources of Americanological expertise apparently agreed that whoever won, there would be an improvement in Soviet-American relations. Carter would have a second honeymoon in which to get the SALT II treaty ratified, while Reagan would, according to the cliché, be another Nixon. There was in Moscow a hope—not a prediction, but a hope—that those traditional elements in U.S. foreign policy represented by Vance might also be represented in the Reagan Administration. Much was made of Reagan's selection of Alexander Haig, a known quantity, to be Secretary of State. Even if Reagan was not another Nixon, Haig at least might be another Kissinger.

As one Soviet observer said, "Maybe Reagan will promise less, but I think he will be able to deliver more."

DETENTE: IRREVERSIBLE OR IRRECOVERABLE?

What they were hoping Reagan would deliver would have been a return to some approximation of the palmy days of détente as it was practiced in the early 1970s. Call it momentum or call it inertia, détente had acquired staying power as a Soviet objective. Khrushchev may have anticipated it, but détente was a policy personally identified with Leonid Brezhnev, the personification of lumbering steadiness. This quality both in Brezhnev and in his reign was partly a reaction to the sudden shifts and reversals, the penchant for improvisation and hare-brained schemes, of his predecessor Khrushchev. But the very fact that Brezhnev forcibly ousted Khrushchev and died on the job eighteen years later suggests that Brezhnev's style was the true Soviet style, and Khrushchev's was something of an aberration.

Most members of the present Politburo came to supreme power during détente. Andropov himself reached the Politburo in 1973, just as détente was reaching its own apogee. So did Gromyko. Détente was the kind of relationship these men were used to, and their careers had thrived in its heyday.

There seems to be no debate in the U.S.S.R. about the value of détente, either in its own time or as a model for a better future. This in itself is curious and perhaps telling. It is easy enough to imagine one of those hardliners we hear so much about making a statement along the following lines: the policies of 1969-74 contributed to the rise of the dissident intelligentsia (however dramatically and tragically the dissidents may have fallen since then); it fostered the rise of anti-Communist Great Russian nationalism or what might be called "Solzhenitsynism" (however much its namesake himself despises détente for his own reasons); and détente contributed to the infestation of Eastern Europe and the U.S.S.R. itself with corrupting alien cultural and ideological influences, unrest in Poland, the opportunity for Nicolae Ceauşescu, the president of Rumania, to shield his renegade foreign policy from the imposition of discipline by Moscow, and other thoroughly unwelcome developments. Indeed, these arguments, or anticipations of them, may once have been voiced by the likes of Pyotr Shelest (the Ukrainian Party chief whom Brezhnev dismissed from the Politburo in 1972, apparently for opposing the first Moscow summit) and other nearly forgotten figures. But they have long since been silenced, and there are no audible echoes of them now.

The Soviets seem united in their nostalgia for détente for reasons that are partly benign and partly less so. Détente entailed potential long-term benefits in trade, credits, and access to Western technology. Détente meant not just the lessening of tensions between the superpowers, but reduced competitiveness on the American side. According to Arnold Horelick, who is director of the newly formed Center for the Study of Soviet International Behavior run by the Rand Corporation and the University of California at Los Angeles: "History has taught Soviet leaders that in such an environment [détente], the risk of unwanted violent confrontation with the U.S. is lessened; that there is a more propitious domestic environment in the U.S. for unilateral arms restraint and hence a better chance for the U.S.S.R. to preserve or even enlarge hard-won gains without racing harder; that there is a higher U.S. tolerance threshold for Soviet expansionism in the Third World; and that there are better prospects for deriving economic benefits from the West."*

One monument to détente—as controversial as the policy itself—is the Final Act of the Conference on Security and Cooperation in Europe signed in Helsinki in 1975. The myth persists among critics of détente that the principal effect of the Helsinki Final Act was to secure international acceptance of Soviet hegemony over Eastern Europe. In fact, nothing of the kind is

*In a discussion paper for the Council study group.

contained in the document—in the text, between the lines or otherwise. What is, however, very explicit is Soviet acceptance of an obligation to respect a long list of human and civil rights. While the U.S.S.R. has observed those mainly in the breach, its leaders must have known that by signing the Final Act, they were giving their adversaries a large and useful stick, albeit a paper one. Why, then, did Brezhnev sign it? The answer, as put by Dimitri Simes of the Carnegie Endowment for International Peace, is that doing so "expressed that incongruous craving to have the U.S.S.R. considered as a peaceable and respectable member of the community of nations."*

Except for fleeting examples like "the spirit of Geneva" and "the spirit of Camp David," détente represented the first, last and only time that the two nations have agreed on a positive description of their relationship. That in itself made the Soviets feel that they had achieved the permanent and internationally acknowledged status of a superpower coequal to the United States; the United States had finally recognized that it must shift from a policy of containment, isolation and encirclement to one of accommodation. A world power cannot, by definition, be contained, isolated or encircled. Global standing meant global reach in the projection of power and influence. Détente meant a sustained opportunity to pursue more ambitious Soviet interests, particularly the cultivation of client states, at relatively low cost, with an implicit license to do so from the other superpower.

It was by no means a foregone conclusion in late 1980 and early 1981 that Ronald Reagan would try to

*In a paper for the Council study group.

revoke that license. Nor was there any conclusive evidence that the Soviets were in a frame of mind to probe or provoke the United States on that score. Quite the contrary, Soviet spokesmen said their leaders were hoping for a *peredyshka*, a respite or breathing period.

All was not going well for the Soviet leaders. Their internal problems were severe and, if anything, becoming worse. The dilemma of Poland was growing more acute, both in and of itself and in its ramifications for the East bloc as a whole. Their Afghan quagmire had become a gnawing preoccupation for the military and an embarrassment for their diplomats and propagandists. The Third World was looking less like a profitable hunting ground and more like a minefield. Their clients faced armed resistance in Angola, Ethiopia, Mozambique, and Cambodia as well as in Afghanistan.

When Alexander Haig remonstrated with Anatoly Dobrynin and Andrei Gromyko on the misbehavior of Soviet-backed regimes, he was told, in effect, "Don't complain to us; they're sovereign states." This response may have been cynical, but it may also have hinted that those Third World troublemakers about whom Haig was so concerned were on their own; Soviet backing went only so far; the U.S.S.R. was less willing than before to pay the bills and certainly less willing to cover the risks of progressive, anti-imperialist forces that found themselves in trouble with the United States.

There were signs that the Soviets were coming to terms with the fact that their American competitor was feeling pushed around and was beginning to look for chances to push others around for a change. They had seen the grass-roots opposition to the Panama Canal treaties and SALT II, as well as grass-roots support for the Olympic boycott. It was not enough to write off these and other conservative backlashes as the spasms of reactionary elements in ruling circles. The nerves twitching in the American body politic suggested a new mood in the country, one that seemed to support the proposition that the United States had given away too much, put up with too much, and ought to start looking for ways to turn the tables.

What this new mood might mean in practice was something that the Soviet leaders would probably just as soon not have found out. They preferred to consolidate their gains and hold potential adversaries at arm's length while they attended to domestic problems and explored the possibility of lessening tension with the United States. A breathing period would also have allowed them to make a virtue of a necessity. Attractive opportunities for expansion were scarce, and trouble-spots were proliferating.

Central America was a case in point, not an exception. Here there was a marked contrast between the view from Moscow and the view from Washington. The Reagan Administration, and Haig in particular, came into office convinced that the Soviets were about to test the mettle of the new American leadership in Central America. Soviet spokesmen protested vigorously, and plausibly, that this was untrue. Events in that region had acquired what good Marxists like to call "an internal dynamic of their own." The Sandinistas had already triumphed in Nicaragua, with at least as much passive help from the United States as active help from the U.S.S.R. and its surrogates; the Salvadoran insurgents were emboldened not by control officers in Moscow but by the triumph of their comrades in Managua; Fidel Castro had reason to hope that a version of his own revolution might finally take root on the mainland of the isthmus.

But the Soviets themselves were not about to challenge the U.S. directly in a region so clearly its sphere of influence. In conversations with Americans through much of 1981 and 1982, the Soviets used Central America to score debating points about their problems in Central Asia. "You see how upset your government is over a region close to its borders? Now you know how we feel about Afghanistan." Significantly, Soviets did not accompany these remarks with threats that the U.S.S.R. might increase its Central American mischief-making in retaliation for U.S. support of the Afghan guerrillas.

Whether Washington was willing to give the Soviets the breathing period they professed to want was initially hard to determine. Presidential rhetoric was extraordinarily harsh. Reagan used his first press conference to call the U.S.S.R. a nation ruled by men who "reserve unto themselves the right to commit any crime, to lie, to cheat." In May 1981, Reagan told an audience of West Point plebes that the U.S.S.R. was an "evil force"; in June 1982, he denounced Soviet "tyranny" in a speech at the United Nations; he told a conference of Christian fundamentalists in Orlando, Florida, that the U.S.S.R. was the "focus of evil in the modern world . . . an evil empire."*

But the Soviet leaders had been called names before by American leaders, and if they were listening carefully—which they certainly were—they also heard Reagan's appeal to Brezhnev, in September 1981, for a

*See Appendix.

"framework of respect" and Alexander Haig's repeated calls for a relationship based on "restraint and reciprocity."

Still, there was an intensity to the denunciations and a distinctly hollow ring to the conciliatory counterpoints, at least to Soviet ears. A Soviet specialist on the United States commented, "We're used to harsh rhetoric. We are not incapable of engaging in it ourselves when we feel it justified. We're used to hearing American presidents talk like schizophrenics. With Carter, it was always interesting to read a speech and say, 'Aha, Vance wrote this one.' Or, 'Here's a paragraph from Brzezinski.' But we have done what you might call 'content analysis' of Reagan statements over the past couple years, and we feel quite sure that the man speaking at West Point and Orlando was, so to say, the real Reagan."

American opinion, on the whole, was willing to give the real Reagan the benefit of the doubt. There was something refreshing in the new President's approach. As the Russians might put it, he called things by their own names. He may have been impolitic, but he was not wrong. After all, the Soviets *do* lie, cheat, and reserve the right to commit any crime; they do preside over the last great empire on earth; and many aspects of their behavior, both toward their own people and toward those of other lands, are so offensive and threatening to the democratic and human values that evil is not an outrageous characterization of them.

There was a sense that Reagan had indeed turned over a new leaf, closing the chapter in American foreign policy in which Marine helicopters tried to rescue Americans from embattled embassies in far-off places— successfully in Saigon, unsucessfully in Tehran, but ignominiously in both cases. Here was a new President who may have tapped into recuperative powers that many Americans feared their nation had lost. And if the Soviets had underestimated those powers, just as many Americans had done, then too bad for the Soviets.

Outside as well as inside the Administration, many thought they saw signs that Reagan's hard line might eventually be having a salutary effect on Soviet international behavior. It was argued that Reagan should be given his due; he had gotten the Soviets' attention by committing the United States to a major defense buildup that seemed to have bipartisan support. The Kremlin leaders were taking Reagan seriously; clearly they were proceeding with caution.

Most of the evidence was negative—dogs that were not barking. Soviet expansion had been slowed; embittered and impacted as the Soviet-American relationship was, it was also remarkably free of full-scale crises. During 1982, for example, there were three major wars: in the Persian Gulf, in Lebanon, and in the Falkland Islands, but none had become a superpower confrontation.

The most notable case was the Middle East. In 1973, at the height of détente, the Yom Kippur War had brought the United States and the Soviet Union to a showdown involving large-scale Soviet resupply of the Arabs and a global American military alert. Yet nine years later, when relations were terrible, Moscow and Washington held their breath and eyed each other nervously during the Israeli invasion of Lebanon. More to the point, the Soviets seemed to take a major setback lying down. Their Syrian clients' MiGs and SAMs were pummeled by the Israelis with virtual impunity. It suddenly became conventional wisdom in Washington that the Soviets were showing "restraint." And as everyone knew, restraint was what the Soviets were supposed to show in response to the new American policy. Therefore it followed that American policy was working.

This view may have been based on a misinterpretation of the Soviet desire for a breathing space as a Soviet retreat in the face of a tough, new American démarche. Administration officials asserted that there was a real connection between American and Soviet policies, but it is not so clear, particularly in hindsight. As noted, the Soviets had their own reasons for reducing their foreign adventurism. Domestic imperatives were asserting themselves; during much of the period in question they were preoccupied with a leadership succession; they were bogged down in Afghanistan and distracted in Poland; they were reassessing their strategy in the Third World and re-evaluating the competition. But reassessment and re-evaluation are, by definition, inconclusive while they are going on. Whatever restraint, uncertainty, and even passivity the U.S.S.R. may have displayed during that period did not mean its leaders had concluded that the correlation of forces had permanently shifted against them or that the most prudent course in the long run was to cut their losses in a new set of arrangements with the United States on American terms.

Quite the contrary. Breathing space, reassessment and re-evaluation all suggest an interlude, different in the tone and direction of events from what came before, but perhaps different from what would come after. Yet there was a tendency in the Administration, tinged with self-congratulation and wishful thinking, to see the Soviet desire for a breathing space as evidence that the Soviets were on the run.

That judgment was, at the very least, premature, and it is not supported by subsequent events. In the Middle East, the Soviets may not have been so much lying down as lying low—letting the Israelis get drawn into a situation in which they would be militarily overextended, politically isolated and a burden to their American backers. While the Soviets did nothing to save the Syrian MiGs and SAMs during the attack, they were quick to replace the ones that had been destroyed and to use the incident to increase their influence in the region. A year after the Israeli attack on Lebanon, Moscow's situation had clearly improved, compared to Washington's. Israel was in disarray. Lebanon was on the brink of de facto partition, much of it under Syrian control; whatever troubles the Soviet dog was having with its Syrian tail were nothing compared to the murderous quandary in which the United States found itself in Lebanon by late 1983.

In short, the Soviets may well not have been cowed by U.S. policy at all. Rather, they may have been waiting to see what opportunities and challenges that policy would present.

GOING OVER REAGAN'S HEAD

Meanwhile, Soviet specialists on the United States— *institutchiki* and government officials alike—indicated they were also waiting to see how the American rhetoric meshed with policy. They were particularly interested in the new burst of talk out of Washington about linkage. Reagan and Haig were then vowing to make linkage a practical, punitive instrument of policy. But when, under pressure from American farmers, Reagan lifted the grain embargo—the major example of linkage that the new Administration inherited from Carter—it became clear that linkage was going nowhere.

The Administration's attempt to punish the Soviets for their imposition of martial law in Poland by imposing sanctions against the Soviet natural gas pipeline project was resisted by the American business community and created new tensions between Washington and Western Europe. Reagan's eventual decision to abandon the policy was noted in Moscow as an indication, in the pedantic formulation of a Foreign Ministry official, that "not even Ronald Reagan is totally immune to the realism imposed by reality itself."

At the same time, however, the Soviets were beginning to express impatience with the overall tenor of American policy. There had been no let-up in what Georgi Arbatov—the director of the Institute for the Study of the U.S.A. and Canada, and Moscow's leading Americanologist—called "threats and insults." In mid-1982, Soviet spokesmen began saying in effect that their government was at its wits' end with the Reagan Administration; the Kremlin doubted it was possible to do business with the United States under its current management.

These themes were certainly intended to exploit differences among various elements within the Administration and within the Western alliance. There was no way of telling whether they also reflected a conclusion at the higher reaches of the Soviet leadership that the

Reagan Administration was impossible to deal with. Yet even if the Kremlin was in some sense on the brink of giving up on the Reagan Administration, it was at pains to say that a breakdown in relations cost the Americans far more than it would the Soviets. The Kremlin's tone was more rueful than angry, and it deliberately avoided any implication that the U.S.S.R. felt unduly threatened or even uncomfortable.

That seemed to be the message delivered in an October 1982 speech by Konstantin Chernenko, who was then a leading candidate to succeed Brezhnev (and who would emerge in February 1984 as successor to Andropov): "For almost two years, the U.S. rulers have been 'flexing their muscles.' For almost two years, abuse directed at the Soviet Union and the other socialist states has been coming out of Washington. . . . But what has Washington achieved?" The answer, Chernenko continued, was that the United States was hurting itself in the eyes of the rest of the world.

As the Soviets hinted that they might simply hunker down and wait for a new Administration, it was their own leadership that changed. When Brezhnev died and Andropov succeeded him, the negotiators in Geneva abruptly backed away from their threats of a walkout, and other spokesmen muffled their expressions of terminal frustration with Washington. Once again, the Soviets seemed to be in quest of a breathing space.

Early in 1983, the familiar representatives of the institutes trooped to the usual conferences in North America and Western Europe. Their message, as articulated in February, in private by one of the best-known and most respected members of that band, was: "Your government hasn't been paying attention to the signals ours has been sending. We want to buckle down to problems that have nothing to do with the zero-sum game between us in the international arena or in the military sphere. Why do you think Andropov is giving all these speeches about the need for discipline in our society and economy? Partly he's talking to our own people, but he's also talking to yours; he's saying *that's* what he wants to concentrate on."

There were new variations on Chernenko's theme of the previous autumn: the United States was, for its own perverse reasons, singlehandedly obstructing progress and rebuffing Soviet overtures; the resulting stagnation, while undesirable, was no skin off the Soviet Union's nose. The implication was that sooner or later, and perhaps later, the United States would realize the error of its ways and come around. Vadim Zagladin, a high Central Committee official, told a Hungarian television interviewer in April 1983, "We have always striven for [better relations], but there is no such striving whatever on the other side. This is a fact that I am forced to note. . . . *But this does not greatly afflict us. We would like to reach a settlement with this Administration, but if it does not want it, that is its problem."* [Italics added.]

The steady, deliberate nurturing and exploitation of the Reagan Administration's problem was rapidly becoming the principal objective of Soviet policy. Ideally, the Soviets may have preferred an improvement in the relationship, but a continued deterioration was not without its compensations and its opportunities. East-West tensions generated West-West tensions. Already in the mid- and late 1970s, the Soviets had seen that the West Europeans and the Americans were parting company on détente. The Soviets could see how unenthusiastic America's European allies were about increased defense spending and post-Afghanistan sanctions. When the United States lifted its grain embargo and retreated quickly from its pipeline sanctions, the Kremlin saw at least two encouraging instances of Washington's anti-Soviet line buckling under pressure from voters and congressmen at home and from partners abroad.

Thus the Soviets have been looking more and more for ways to influence Reagan indirectly, through his constituencies and through the constituencies of his allies.

The Soviets would no doubt love to manipulate American domestic politics. If they could find a way to tip the 1984 election to Reagan's opponent—*any* opponent, most probably (unless, of course, it were a Republican challenger to Reagan's right)—they would almost certainly do so. But they have no such opportunity, and there are definite risks in attempting to manufacture one.

Whatever consolation they may have derived from the collapse of the grain embargo and the pipeline sanctions, they have also seen Reagan work wonders in his handling of Congress and the public on a variety of issues. He has had trouble sustaining support for an American military presence in Lebanon and for U.S. intervention in Central America, but his explicitly anti-Soviet/anti-Cuban invasion of Grenada actually boosted his popularity in the public opinion polls.

A serious Soviet-American showdown in 1984 might heighten the American electorate's fears about war and make the voters more receptive to the Democratic challenger as a peace candidate. But it is just as possible that a crisis might have the opposite effect of rallying Americans not only around the flag but around their President, bolstering his bid for re-election. In any event, the Soviets are unlikely to stage a crisis simply to see what its political effect might be in the United States. They would be gambling not just on the outcome of the election, but on the outcome of the crisis itself, and that would be as out of character as it would be reckless.

Besides, they have probably not made up their mind about what they are dealing with in the United States: is it just Reaganism, or is it a new, far more deep-seated, systemic phenomenon that they will have to cope with for years, no matter who the President is?

All the more reason, therefore, for them to concentrate on Europe. There the opportunities for pressure and manipulation are more evident, less ambiguous, and less risky. Traditionally, the Soviets have sought to keep their all-important Western front quiet by a combination of intimidation and overtures aimed at the Western leaders as well as by manipulating Western public opinion. But during the Reagan Administration, public opinion seemed to become the Soviets' principal target while direct superpower diplomacy took second place to the propaganda effort.

If the burghers, hausfraus, clerics, students, and Social Democratic politicians of West Germany would put enough pressure on their government in Bonn, perhaps that government in turn would put enough pressure on Washington to rein in the Administration.

"We can expect sober forces once again to take the upper hand," Zagladin said in his April 1983 interview with Hungarian television. "Or rather not so much that they will take the upper hand, but that political movements will push them into the forefront. We won't do the pushing; political movements there [in the West] will do it."

In fact, the Soviets did a good deal of pushing, particularly in West Germany early in 1983, where they hoped to influence the March elections. Andropov invited the Social Democratic opposition leader, Hans-Jochen Vogel, to Moscow and dangled all kinds of carrots in front of him: arms-control concessions, new solutions to the old problem of divided German families, economic opportunities galore—if only the Federal Republic would turn its back on the U.S. missiles. Shortly afterward, Gromyko, leaving the carrots at home, traveled to Bonn with a big stick, threatening his hosts with dire military and political consequences if the deployments went ahead.

It was a classic case of what is, from the standpoint of the West, one of the most welcome features of Soviet foreign policy: the proclivity for overplaying its hand in a way that benefits the other side. Just when it looked as though the Soviet peace offensive in Europe might be getting somewhere in promoting a Nordic nuclear free zone, a Soviet "whiskey-class" submarine with nuclear weapons aboard can be counted on to run onto the rocks in Sweden's territorial waters while on a spying mission against that neutral nation's most sensitive naval facilities. Likewise, just when it looked as though the Soviets might indeed be helping the Social Democrats in West Germany, they managed to make Vogel, the Social Democratic candidate for Chancellor, look like a patsy, Gromyko like a ham-fisted bully, and the conservative, staunchly pro-American incumbent Helmut Kohl like a tough, principled patriot and champion of the Western alliance.

There is no question that the Soviets would have liked to see the West Europeans repudiate the deployment altogether, thus ridding them of an additional military threat and, more important, encouraging divisive recriminations within NATO for years to come. However, there is also no question that with the beginning of deployment on schedule at the end of 1983, the U.S.S.R. had sustained a major political defeat. In some ways, it was a self-inflicted defeat insofar as the Soviets had inadvertently contributed to Kohl's victory in the election. Perhaps their principal error had been to define their effort in all-or-nothing terms: either to win by stopping deployment altogether, or to lose if preliminary deployment were to begin.

At the same time, however, while the Soviets clearly mishandled their side of the zero-sum game in Europe, it may turn out that Washington totted up its own gains too quickly and too complacently, for the game is not over. The Soviets can, and doubtless do, still hope that NATO is in for a traumatic experience nonetheless. If the initial deployments are followed by months and perhaps years of political debate in Europe over whether additional missiles are still to come, and whether the ones already in place are to stay, the result could be lasting bruises on the solidarity of the alliance, crippling its ability to respond to future pressures that the U.S.S.R. might exert.

The victories of Kohl in Germany and Margaret Thatcher in Britain have tended to obscure another much more ominous development: two of the largest, most important opposition parties in Western Europe, British Labour and the West German Social Democrats, have moved far to the left and adopted platforms that are not just anti-deployment but very close to being anti-NATO. The good news is that their leftward lurch may keep them in the opposition; the bad news is that even in the opposition they can cause a lot of trouble for Washington and the alliance; and the even worse news is that given the volatility of European politics, it would be reckless to assume that they will never be back in power.

In the case of China policy, the Soviets also saw a chance to go over Reagan's head. During the first years of his Administration, while he was trying to reconcile his old feelings of friendship for Taiwan with his new appreciation of the importance of the People's Republic as a counterweight to the U.S.S.R., the Soviets had an opportunity to improve their own relations with the People's Republic—an effort which Brezhnev personally joined in his last months. Partly in reaction to what they saw as Washington's retrograde policies, the Chinese were expressing new interest in reducing tensions with the U.S.S.R. and in striking a posture of equidistance from the superpowers.

But here, too, the Soviets may have made their move too late, with too little—and, once again, too awkwardly. Meanwhile, the Reagan Administration was finally bringing its China policy into line with that of its predecessors. Thus by mid-1983, the Chinese, despite their rhetoric about equidistance, would continue to tilt toward the United States in security matters as well as trade.

Significantly, those hopeful signs between Washington and Beijing coincided with the first, slight indications in early and mid-1983 that better relations might be developing between Washington and Moscow. George Shultz was reported by the press to be in more regular contact with Ambassador Dobrynin; other American diplomats were traveling to Moscow with the announced intention of engaging the Soviets in a constructive dialogue; White House and State Department officials spoke cautiously of a possible breakthrough in the arms talks.

Such was the dynamic of the triangular relationship: the People's Republic was willing to draw closer to the United States at a time when a rapprochement was less likely to be interpreted by the Soviets as a maneuver directed against them. When the leaders of the PRC agreed to let Secretary of Defense Caspar Weinberger visit in late 1983 and to permit an exchange of visits by heads-of-government in 1984, they apparently believed that a Soviet-American summit was also in the offing. The Chinese were encouraging better Sino-American relations on the mistaken assumption that Soviet-American relations would be getting better, too. They were taken aback by the sudden, precipitous downturn between Moscow and Washington in the fall of 1983. That was probably one reason for their equivocation over the Korean airliner affair and their refusal to join the American-led chorus of condemnation.

The Soviets, meanwhile, had been propagandizing about a "substantial détente" with the PRC that was "irreversible, significant and indisputable." A deputy foreign minister, Mikhail Kapitsa, visited Beijing in September 1983 and spoke of "a new basis" for Sino-Soviet rapprochement. As Reagan himself prepared to visit China in the spring of 1984, the Soviets denounced the militarization of U.S. policy in Asia, thus playing on Chinese unease about being drawn in on the

U.S. side in the triangular game. But the Chinese were clearly playing their own hand. Ideally, they would like to have both superpowers vying for favor in the Middle Kingdom. They were glad to be on the receiving end of an apparent Soviet peace initiative, not least because the United States was sure to react with a burst of anxiety about whether it was losing influence on China and therefore adjust its own course so as not to be outflanked by the Soviets.

THE HARDWARE CHALLENGE

Up to this point in their analysis, those Soviets who had originally preferred Reagan over Carter might well have felt vindicated. In some respects, Carter might have seemed more troublesome and obnoxious than Reagan was turning out to be. After all, in the grain embargo and the Olympic boycott Carter had taken concrete measures intended to strike at the heart of Soviet economic interests and prestige. Reagan never went so far. Carter, goaded by Brzezinski, had played the China card for all it was worth and perhaps more; Reagan, the friend of Taiwan and diehard anti-Communist, had taken nearly two years even to pick up the China card, and he was playing it with neither great skill nor great enthusiasm.

In early 1983, Dimitri Simes believed that "the prevailing view of the U.S.S.R.'s America-watchers finds Reagan either unable or unwilling (or both) to undertake policies which could genuinely lead to a possibility of direct military confrontation between the superpowers." Arnold Horelick agreed: in Soviet eyes, the Reagan Administration was "distinctly hostile [but] not incautious . . . implacably hostile in its convictions and openly expressed goals, yet no more aggressive in its behavior than any of its more 'moderate' predecessors and much less so than some."*

Yet at about this same time, early 1983, Soviet commentators were beginning to project a very different, much harsher view of the Reagan Administration than the one attributed to them by even the most astute American experts. Reagan, they were saying, had turned out to be far worse than Carter, far worse than any other President with whom they had ever been confronted. They were also talking in much more alarming, even alarmist, terms than their American counterparts about the state of the relationship and the danger of conflict.

Two features of the Administration's policy toward the U.S.S.R. seemed to upset them especially. One was what might be called the hardware of that policy—the Administration's apparent determination to regain military superiority; the other was the software—its determination to regain the ideological offensive against the U.S.S.R., to foment trouble among Soviet clients and within the Soviet empire, and even to tamper with the inner workings of the Kremlin itself.

★

When two states distrust and despise each other, they naturally think a lot about matters of military

*As before, these citations are from Simes's and Horelick's papers for the study group.

wherewithal. The more they dwell on the danger each poses to the other, the more they think of ways to do each other in, the more each becomes obsessed with military security. Because of the fundamental incompatibility between the superpowers' interests and values, there has always been some level on which they have been preparing for war—and thus, each by its own lights, deterring war. Sometimes the undercurrent of militarization in the relationship is suppressed, sometimes sublimated, sometimes brought to the surface. In such an antagonism, there probably will always be a dimension of mutual intimidation; but under Reagan, this dimension took priority over all others, in Soviet eyes as well as American.

There were many attempts by the two powers to compete for influence with third countries by such nonmilitary means as political manipulation and propaganda, but the issues involved were—directly or indirectly, explicitly or implicitly—still military. In Europe, all other questions of East-West and West-West relations alike were subordinated to the controversy over new missiles for NATO; in Central America, the debate was over Soviet and Cuban arms for leftist guerrillas in El Salvador and American arms for counterrevolutionaries in Nicaragua; Washington tried to engage the People's Republic of China in a dialogue on arms sales.

The Reagan Administration deemed Soviet-American diplomacy suspect almost by definition, since even on the chilliest terms, diplomacy presumes that a degree of civilized discourse and behavior is possible. Where diplomacy and military competition overlap is arms control. Therefore, not surprisingly, the Reagan

Administration and the Kremlin approached arms-control negotiations as a way not of regulating or ameliorating the competition between them so much as pressing for advantage against each other. Diplomacy itself was militarized.

For the Soviets, the most important achievement of the Brezhnev era was equality, or parity, between the superpowers. They say as much, and they say it over and over. Détente, in their vocabulary, translates not just as the reduction of tensions between the superpowers but as the mutual acceptance of equality between them. The Soviets define parity largely, indeed almost exclusively, in military terms. After all, what other terms are there? Certainly the U.S.S.R. cannot claim to compete with the United States economically; its values and lifestyle offer little to its own people, to say nothing of the rest of the world.

Because of the supreme importance that the Soviets attach to the preservation of military equality and, just as important, to American acquiescence in that preservation, arms control has a sanctity of its own. Arms control, in their eyes, is the regulation of military competition and the codification of parity. Soviets evince none of the ambivalence that afflicts Americans on the subject. That is not surprising. For the Soviets, the arms-control agreements of the 1970s meant that they had come from behind and caught up with the United States; for many Americans, those agreements meant the same thing, but with an implication that was as unwelcome as it was inescapable: the United States had lost superiority. Whether the new state of affairs should be called parity or inferiority was one of the principal points of contention in the great debate over national security that has been going on for the past few years, but almost no one denies that the Soviet Union's gain was the U.S.'s loss.

With Reagan in the White House, the Soviets came to see their achievement of military parity at risk. Meanwhile, Andropov, to establish his legitimacy as Brezhnev's successor, had to consolidate the achievement. Or to put it negatively, he could not be the Soviet leader who "lost parity."

The challenge was more apparent in American conduct of the bilateral arms-control process than unilateral American defense policy. Reagan's much-ballyhooed strategic modernization was not so different from what his predecessors had pursued. The MX, the Trident II, the cruise missile program, the Stealth Bomber were all inheritances from the Carter Administration. The only exception was the B-1, which Carter canceled and Reagan revived. At the same time, however, Carter intended to deploy more MXs than Reagan did.

Nor was there much that was all that new in U.S. military doctrine. When Alexander Haig mused about a "demonstration" shot (setting off a thermonuclear explosion to impress the Soviets with American willingness to use nuclear weapons against their forces), when members of the Administration said provocatively that a nuclear war could be fought and won, and when leaks appeared in the press about the Pentagon Defense Guidance Plan (a suddenly not-so-secret document signed by Secretary Weinberger calling on the United States to develop the capability to "prevail" in a nuclear war), the Soviets probably attended the furor more with a smirk than with shock. Debatable as these various statements were, they did not represent a revolution or even much of a revision in American strategic thinking. Rather, they attempted to refine nuclear doctrine as it had evolved under Robert McNamara, James Schlesinger, Zbigniew Brzezinski and Harold Brown. Loose talk about nuclear weapons and nuclear war probably created a good deal more anxiety in Western Europe and in the United States than in the Kremlin. In fact, the Soviets may even have welcomed these statements as an opportunity to make propaganda at America's expense with their own proposals for a joint pledge not to be the first to resort to the use of nuclear weapons.

It was in arms control that the Kremlin found itself dealing with something truly new and deeply disturbing. The Administration was advancing tenaciously and unabashedly a number of propositions that profoundly offended and alarmed the U.S.S.R. Never before had the United States espoused any of these ideas individually, let alone as a mutually reinforcing package:

1. The United States was militarily inferior to the Soviet Union.

2. In the past, arms control had contributed to American military inferiority and, if continued, would have locked the United States permanently into second place. For the sake of disarmament, the United States gave up military options that it should have protected through rearmament, and it compounded that mistake by letting the Soviets keep open all their options, and all their assembly lines.

3. Because the United States was behind, and because arms control was partly to blame, the best course was to suspend bilateral bargaining and concentrate on a unilateral American rearmament. Once the United

re-established equality or, better yet, a "margin
...city," it could resume talks and negotiate from
strength.

4. If forced by political expediency to engage in
arms control, the United States must find a way of
pursuing an arms buildup simultaneously, and it must
give priority to the buildup on its own side.

5. In order to be meaningful and salutary, arms control must feature reductions, and the deeper the reductions, the better the agreement for U.S. interests and
for the stability of the Soviet-American nuclear balance.

6. The United States must insist on drastic cutbacks
in the most modern, potent Soviet weapons already deployed; no comparable reductions should be considered
in existing American forces. Arms control could—indeed, must—result in nothing less than a top-to-bottom
overhaul of the Soviet arsenal, and to accomplish
changes in the nuclear balance that the United States
had not been able to bring about by dint of its own
defense programs.

The logic of such a transparently one-sided set of
objectives was straightforward enough: if the United
States was not going to build up to a position of
strength from which it could negotiate in the future,
then the Soviet Union must build down to a position
that the United States would recognize as equality.

For many years, American analysts had worried
about the composition of the Soviet arsenal, particularly
its heavily MIRVed land-based ballistic missiles, which
are, in the view of many Western analysts, potential
first-strike weapons. There had been attempts in
SALT to include in various proposals inducements for

the Soviets to "move out to sea"—that is, develop more submarines and fewer large land-based weapons.

Not until the Reagan Administration, however, did the predominant and avowed purpose of arms control become virtually to dictate to the U.S.S.R. an entirely new sort of arsenal, one more to American liking and one that required that the Soviets scrap their latest, most cost-effective, most powerful, and most highly valued weapons.

For more than a decade, American military planners and political leaders had worried about the loss of superiority, the achievement of parity by the Soviet Union, and the danger that unless the United States improved its defenses, the Soviets would pull ahead in the future. There were analysts in the back rooms of the Carter Pentagon and members of the National Security Council staff who feared that the future had already arrived. Never before, however, had a President made pessimism about the existing state of military balance the basis of his world view and of his program.

At a news conference in March 1982, Reagan said, "The truth of the matter is that on balance the Soviet Union does have a definite margin of superiority." He and Secretary of Defense Weinberger repeated that assessment many times. The Soviets had heard American leaders and would-be leaders cry alarm before about various gaps—missile gaps, bomber gaps, megaton gaps—but never before had they been faced with a U.S. executive branch that based its policies both for defense and for arms control on the premise that the U.S.S.R. was significantly ahead in most important measures of power.

For public consumption, when receiving visitors at the institutes or sending spokesmen to attend conferences in the West, the Soviets asserted that the United States had undergone a kind of reactionary restoration; its leadership had fallen into the hands of "ruling circles" that had never liked détente, never accepted parity, and were as nostalgic for the Pax Americana as Soviet ruling circles were for détente on their terms. They dismissed Americans' laments about inferiority as a smokescreen behind which sinister forces were trying to regain superiority.

Privately, however, quite a few Soviets conceded that perhaps key people in the Reagan Administration honestly believed what they were saying, and that the self-perception of U.S. inferiority had worked its way into the prevailing American mentality. Sophisticated Soviets even conceded that perhaps they had failed to appreciate how sensitive the United States would be to losing its military superiority; perhaps their side should have taken more seriously what one spokesman called "your Pearl Harbor syndrome"—that is, the perception (or, in the Soviet view, misperception) that Soviet weapons now threatened the United States with surprise attack. But, these Soviets hastened to add, this perception was "objectively" wrong, politically unacceptable, because it made the United States all the less accommodating to Soviet "rights" and dangerous, because it led Washington to pursue policies that were one-sided and provocative.

Early in the first round of the Strategic Arms Reduction Talks (START), a Soviet negotiator delivered a lecture to his American counterpart: "It doesn't really matter whether your leaders cynically *say* the U.S. is weaker than we are and must catch up, or whether they *believe* what they say. The result is the same. They want more for themselves even while they try to take away from us what we already have. Normal relations in general, and arms control in particular, are possible only when both of us accept that we are proceeding from a starting point of equality as well as proceeding toward an end point of equality. The Reagan Administration pays lipservice to the latter but makes no bones about rejecting the former."

Whatever else it claimed or sought in its own conduct of START and Intermediate-range Nuclear Forces (INF) talks on weapons in Europe, the Soviet Union was determined to reject the insinuation that the U.S.S.R. must pay a penalty for having taken advantage of the United States in the past: hence the constant protests that the U.S. proposals were unequal in that they required much greater sacrifices in existing forces on the Soviet side than on the American side; hence also the constant charge that the United States was using arms-control negotiations as a cover for its effort to "catch up"—by which the Soviets meant surpass the U.S.S.R.—in the arms race; hence the Soviets' repeated complaints, in Geneva and elsewhere, that the Reagan Administration was not "serious" about arms control.

Earlier Administrations had sought to put their own stamp on arms control, but sooner rather than later they came around to picking up where their predecessors had left off. Earlier Administrations had also discovered the futility of trying to conduct negotiations in the absence of progress toward establishing a broader political dialogue. Arms control had been buffeted by the upheavals of American domestic politics before, but it had always survived and advanced—until Reagan came along.

The foundation for SALT was laid in the Johnson Administraton. The formal opening of those negotiations was delayed in 1968 by the Soviet invasion of Czechoslovakia, which coincided with an American presidential campaign. A Democratic President who had been largely discredited in foreign policy gave way to a Republican one who had made his career largely on a reputation for implacable anti-Sovietism. Once in office, Richard Nixon circled the idea of SALT cautiously before deciding to make it his own. But when he moved, it was with dispatch and skill, and with considerable fidelity to the groundwork that he had inherited. When Nixon was succeeded by Gerald Ford, SALT II was a work in progress. Ford met with Brezhnev at Vladivostok in November 1974 to sign an accord that did not yield a treaty but served to tide the negotiations over the disruptions caused by the change of leadership in the United States.

Jimmy Carter came to power convinced that he could leapfrog over the unfinished SALT II into a much more ambitious agreement that achieved drastic reductions, largely in Soviet forces. The attempt was the so-called Comprehensive Proposal of March 1977, and the result was a debacle. Carter's Secretary of State, Cyrus Vance, was rudely rebuffed on a visit to Moscow; he was told in no uncertain terms that the Soviet leadership did not have to start from scratch every time a new president arrived in the White House with a new idea. The Carter Administration regrouped and came back to the Soviets with a proposal that preserved and improved on what had already been accomplished in SALT II, and the result was the treaty signed in 1979.

Ronald Reagan was the first president who willfully and persistently set about to break with the past. Among the many criticisms he and his aides had of the Carter Administraton was that it had taken *nyet* for an answer in March 1977; if only Carter and Vance had stuck with the Comprehensive Proposal, the Soviets might have come around. Some Soviet spokesmen inadvertently encouraged this line of speculation by dropping hints in 1981 that the Comprehensive Proposal had failed in part because it was sprung on the Kremlin by surprise. The Soviets meant to stress that arms control should combine continuity with quiet diplomacy, but members of the Reagan Administration inferred that an ambitious new departure of their own might succeed if they stood their ground and gave the Kremlin a chance to reconsider its initial rejection.

As it happened, the Soviet rejection of Washington's START proposal stiffened over time, at least in part because the American position itself grew steadily less negotiable. The opening proposal was for two limits in the near term on total ballistic missile warheads and on those based on land, and in the longer term, a low limit on ballistic missile throw-weight. This was already unacceptable to the Soviets, since the limit on land-based warheads alone would force them to reduce drastically the number of ICBM warheads they were allowed under SALT II, while it would actually permit the United States to increase its forces. While the Soviets were laying out their rejection, the American side came forward with what could only seem like an insult added to an attempted injury: "collateral restraints" that would require the Soviets to reduce specific weapons systems to stipulated, very low levels.

Then, in the fall of 1982, came a proposal for an "inventory limit" on *un*deployed ICBMs. This was seen by the American side as insurance against the Soviets' being able to hide away huge numbers of extra ICBMs that they could use to "reconstitute" their forces after the fifth or tenth "exchange" in a lengthy nuclear conflict. Such an inventory limit could be verified only with comprehensive, intrusive on-site inspection of production and storage facilities, as well as launch sites.

Even though they were adamant in their rejection of the U.S. proposal, the Soviets had initially adopted a relatively flexible attitude in some respects: they had given up their earlier insistence on the ratification of SALT II as a precondition for a new agreement; they indicated a willingness to accept more significant reductions and more stringent verification measures than they had earlier. For example, they were showing some signs of easing their traditional refusal to accept any kind of on-site inspection. But they were not about to grant the United States the kind of search warrant to look anywhere it wanted from one end of the U.S.S.R. to the other.

The point of American flexibility the Soviets cared about most was limitations on cruise missiles. Cruise missiles threaten to make the U.S.S.R.'s air defense system obsolete. Cruise missiles also symbolize a more general problem—American technological superiority.

The Soviets have an almost mystical faith in American technology as a kind of black magic of which their enemy is master. American microcircuitry is the stuff that military breakthroughs and breakouts are made of. A Soviet diplomat once remarked that his government valued its consulate in San Francisco far more than its embassy in Washington or its mission at the United Nations because of its proximity to Silicon Valley, "where the real action is in your country." He was half-joking, but the remark was telling nonetheless, and perhaps a bit indiscreet in the glimpse it might provide into the priorities of Soviet intelligence-gathering organizations, which are well represented in the San Francisco consulate. (For that reason, among others, Soviet diplomatic personnel were subjected to tighter travel restrictions in late 1983, and Silicon Valley was put out of bounds.)

In addition to seeing the United States protect cruise missiles in its arms control proposals for both INF and START, the Soviets saw it protecting other weapons (the MX ICBM and the Trident II SLBM, as well as the Pershing II IRBM) that could neutralize the Soviet advantage in large, heavily MIRVed ballistic missiles. All these programs proceeded apace while the United States tried to force massive reductions in those very Soviet missiles that the MX and Trident II were meant to counter.

The START proposal, even as amended, was meant to achieve deep reductions in one Soviet weapon system in particular: the 308 SS-18s, the so-called heavies, the monster-MIRVs. This feature of START was doubly offensive to the Soviets: first, because they regarded the SS-18s as king on their side of the chessboard, yet the United States insisted on treating them as pawns; and second, because the Soviets believed that the United States had agreed in effect to leave the heavy missiles alone as part of the 1974 Vladivostok

Accord between Brezhnev and Ford. At that meeting, there was an important trade-off: Brezhnev apparently overcame the objections of some of his military advisers and agreed to drop the previous Soviet demand that "forward-based systems" (primarily American nuclear-capable aircraft in and around Europe) be on the table in SALT II, while Ford and Kissinger agreed to carry over from SALT I into SALT II a freeze on heavy missiles. In practice, that meant leaving the Soviets with a monopoly in heavy missiles, since the U.S. had none, and never planned to have any.

This was the background to the lengthy attack on the American START proposal which Andrei Gromyko made in June 1982 at the United Nations:

"The centerpiece of the American position . . . is that first it is necessary to hold talks on SLBMs and ICBMs [as opposed to bombers and cruise missiles], and the centerpiece of this centerpiece, so to say, is Soviet missiles of a certain type—namely, heavy SS-18s. . . . An agreement was reached [at Vladivostok] that the Soviet Union should retain the missiles I have mentioned above without any restrictions either in the quantitative or the qualitative respect."

Gromyko went on to say that if the Soviet Union were to do what the United States was doing—disregard past agreements and not just start from scratch, but try to concentrate only on the weapons in which it was at a disadvantage—"we could propose, for instance, that the almost three-fold superiority of the U.S. over the Soviet Union in the warheads of SLBMs should be the most destabilizing factor. And we could say, 'Let's discuss that first.' But we do not say that, because we proceed from the assumption that everything was balanced out in the SALT II treaty."

The Reagan Administration, of course, proceeded from the very different assumption that SALT II ratified an imbalance in favor of the U.S.S.R., and that START should redress the imbalance. While the debate over the strategic balance is as legitimate as it is complicated, and while there are plenty of valid points to be made on both sides, the simple fact is that the Soviets would never accept the proposition that SALT II was unequal or that they had upset the balance and must now pay a penalty by giving up their most highly valued weapons.

Hence Andropov's statement on September 28, 1983: "Nor do we see that the American side is willing to handle in earnest the problem of limiting and reducing strategic armaments. In the American capital they are now busy launching the production of ever new systems of these armaments as well. They are to be followed shortly by weapons which may radically alter the notions of strategic stability and the very possibility of effective limitation and reduction of nuclear arms."

The latter reference was, once again, primarily to cruise missiles. To be sure, the double build-down concept that Reagan incorporated into START shortly after Andropov's statement offered tradeoffs between cruise missiles and ballistic warheads. But the various formulas being considered on the American side deliberately inflated the value, or cost, of MIRVs because they were more destabilizing (that is, they were potential instruments of a first strike), while they discounted the cost of cruise missiles (because they were, in the American view, instruments solely of retaliation). Also, the Soviets could see perfectly well that the Administration incorporated the double build-down into its START proposal only under duress, as a way of assuaging the arms-control lobby in the Congress and averting the cancellation of the MX—a weapon that the Soviets feared. Therefore the addition of the double build-down to the American position in Geneva probably did little to alter the Soviet interpretation of the Reagan Administration's intentions in arms control.

In the Intermediate-range Nuclear Forces (INF) talks, too, the bottom line of the U.S. position was an addition to American nuclear forces and a subtraction from the Soviet side of the equation. The Western debate over the Soviet conduct of INF tended to focus on the question of whether the Kremlin believed its own rhetoric that the Pershing II was a first-strike weapon that threatened to decapitate Soviet command-and-control—that is, nullify the ability of the leaders to make war—and whether the Soviets feared the Pershing II more than the other weapon system in the NATO package, Tomahawk ground-launched cruise missiles. The answer probably was that the Soviets feared each for different reasons. The Pershing II might eventually be fitted with multiple (as well as maneuverable) warheads, given a range sufficient to reach Moscow and beyond, and deployed in greater numbers than the 108 called for under the 1979 NATO decision. Also, the Soviets really do fear German fingers anywhere near the nuclear trigger. At the same time, the Soviets almost certainly amplified their own alarm about both weapon systems in order to play on the worries of citizens and opposition politicians in the countries where those missiles were to be deployed. The purpose of the Pershing IIs and Tomahawks was to protect the West

Europeans by countering the threat posed by the SS-20 ballistic missiles that the U.S.S.R. had been deploying since 1977.* But once they began arriving, the new American missiles looked to many Europeans more like a provocation than a protection, and the Soviets did all they could to encourage that anxiety.

Once again, however, as with START, the weapons themselves were not the central issue. The firepower of 572 warheads, while awesome in the absolute, is marginal compared to the firepower of the overall NATO arsenal. The difference between the launch-to-target flight time of a Pershing II based in West Germany and a Minuteman based in North Dakota would hardly make much difference in the deliberations of the Soviet Defense Council over how to respond. And if cruise missiles really can sneak in under Soviet air defenses, their warning time would be zero. As with the weapons on the agenda in START, the Pershing II and Tomahawks were already trundling on their troubled way toward deployment when Reagan took office; he inherited them, and all the headaches that accompanied NATO's 1979 dual-track decision (to prepare for deployment while negotiating on the nuclear balance in Europe).

What probably mattered most to the Soviets was the way Reagan set about negotiating. It was a way that seemed transparently designed to produce a stalemate,

---

*For informed, persuasive, yet necessarily conjectural explanations of why the Soviets felt it necessary to deploy the SS-20s in the first place, see *Nuclear Weapons in Europe*, edited by Andrew Pierre, particularly the chapter by William Hyland, published by the Council on Foreign Relations, 1984; and William Garner's *Soviet Threat Perceptions of NATO's Eurostrategic Missiles*, published by the Atlantic Institute for International Affairs, 1983.

and that was, like START, based on the proposition that equality could be achieved only as a result of what the Soviets saw—and rejected—as "unilateral disarmament" on their part.

It has been frequently asserted that the Soviet approach to INF was every bit as cynical, every bit as "unserious," every bit as much a matter of public relations—rather than real arms control—as the American approach. Maybe so. But there was one intriguing episode which suggests that the Soviets just might have engaged in real bargaining that would have produced a real opportunity for the West. That may have been the significance of the famous but still mysterious "walk-in-the-woods" deal that Paul Nitze worked out with his counterpart, Yuli Kvitsinsky, during a stroll in the forest outside Geneva in July 1982.

That episode has been the object of intense speculation and debate since it became widely known early in 1983.*

The two negotiators agreed to a formula by which the Soviet Union would substantially reduce its SS-20s threatening Western Europe, and the United States would cancel the Pershing II program, proceeding only with cruise missiles. The deal was subsequently repudiated by both the Reagan Administration and the Soviet government. Nitze's critics, inside the Administration and out, have tended to the view that Kvitsinsky and his masters in Moscow were just leading Nitze on to see what concessions he would offer, and that the Soviet side was never serious about the compromise. That is

*The background and aftermath of the incident figure prominently in my forthcoming history of INF and START, *Deadly Gambits*, to be published later this year by Alfred A. Knopf.

possible. But it is also possible that the Soviets may have signaled a willingness to accept some American cruise missiles and reduce Soviet ballistic missiles in Europe in exchange for cancellation of new ballistic missiles on the Western side.

Brezhnev was still alive, but he was dying. As a result of Nitze's initiative, Brezhnev may have been tempted by the prospect of a breakthrough in INF and a last summit. We will never know, for the Reagan Administration rejected what the Soviets surely regarded as the key feature of the deal—the sacrifice of the Pershing II—and signaled its repudiation to Moscow before there was any Soviet response whatsoever.

By the time the Administration was willing and able to offer concessions in INF, nearly another year had passed, and whatever chance of an agreement had existed was now gone. The full-dress presidential speech had now become the standard means by which the two powers advanced their proposals. The result was a game of high-level, high-visibility, high-volume one-upsmanship that made progress behind closed doors at the negotiating table all the more difficult and created the impression that the Soviet-American competition was now a highly public, highly personalized affair between the two leaderships. This was the opposite of summitry.

In this regard, it was significant that the proximate cause of Andropov's watershed statement denouncing the U.S. Administration on September 28, 1983, was Ronald Reagan's presentation two days before of three new "initiatives" (the American euphemism for concessions) in INF. In rejecting those initiatives, Andropov went beyond the issues at hand to denounce what he called the "essence" of the Administration's approach to arms control. The original Zero Option of November 1981 (cancellation of the NATO deployment in exchange for elimination of all SS-20s throughout the U.S.S.R.) and the Interim Solution proposal of May 1983, as amended in September (equal levels of intermediate-range warheads on both sides), both came down to the same thing, according to Andropov: "the proposal to agree, as before, on how many Soviet medium-range missiles should be reduced and how many new American missiles should be deployed in Europe in addition to the nuclear potential already possessed by NATO. In brief, it is proposed that we talk about how to help the NATO bloc upset to its advantage the balance of medium-range nuclear systems in the European zone."

Andropov's claim that a balance existed in Europe was questionable in the extreme, and his suggestion that the United States did not have the right, in concert with its allies, to enhance the collective security of the West was breathtaking in its effrontery. But his characterization of the U.S. proposal was accurate enough. The United States was indeed trying to get the Soviets to build down while it built up to some point that satisfied the American definition of equality. That was truly the essence of the American position in both START and INF.

The substance of arms control is also the substance of the military competition: the negotiators negotiate about the numbers and characteristics of the armaments that make up the two sides' arsenals of last resort and that symbolize the stability of the relationship when it is reduced to measurements of raw power. Arms-control agreements, when they are achieved, tend to be seen by both sides not just as regulations for the competition but also as codifications of equality and as mutual commitments to preserve and honor that equality. Conversely, when agreement is thwarted, each side tends to blame the other for the lack of progress and also to impute to the other side the sinister motive of seeking unilateral advantage (yet another favorite phrase in the lexicon of Soviet grievances).

In authorizing Andropov to denounce not just Reagan's specific proposals but the underlying assumptions and later recalling their negotiators from Geneva and Vienna, the Soviet leaders were dramatizing a conclusion about what they took to be the foundation of American policy: despite all the tactical shifts, rhetorical modulations, internal debates, and conflicting signals that characterized the Reagan Administration's conduct of policy toward the U.S.S.R., the Soviets saw at work an all-too consistent American determination to turn back the clock on military parity and regain for the United States the superiority it had enjoyed before the era of détente.

The START and INF negotiations in Geneva had been among the few institutionalized points of regular, intensive, bilateral contact between the superpowers during the Reagan Administration. When the Soviets decided to act on their apparent conclusion that they could accomplish nothing with this Administration, arms control was the only diplomatic business in which the two countries were still engaged—other than, of course, the exchange of protests and remonstrations. Thus it was the only business available for suspension.

In that sense, the vulnerability of arms control was a function of its durability. It had survived threats of punitive linkage from both sides before, but now the Soviets were looking for a way of dramatizing their contention that a new, more confrontational period in the the the relationship had begun—allegedly at American instigation. The United States, in their view, had conspired with its allies against parity and thus betrayed the spirit of détente; therefore the U.S.S.R. was giving up on détente, too. Arms control was a link with the past that had to be broken, if not forever, then for some time to come.

Throughout this period, the superpowers were still claiming to adhere to the expired SALT I Interim Agreeement on offensive weapons, the SALT I Anti-Ballistic Missile (ABM) treaty and the unratified SALT II treaty. But this position was steadily eroding. The impending deployment of American ground-launched cruise missiles in Europe would make a dead letter of an agreement that accompanied the SALT II treaty. The Soviets called it a violation.

Meanwhile, the Soviets were engaged in a number of activities of their own that called into question their compliance with the agreements. They were making extensive use of codes in the testing of ICBMs and thus playing close to the rather fuzzy margins of what was permissible under SALT II (the treaty banned the use of any codes that impede the other side's ability to verify compliance). They appeared to be developing two new types of ICBM, while only one was permitted under SALT II; and most troubling of all, they were operating a large radar facility in Siberia that strained even the most lenient interpretation of what was allowed under SALT I. These were among the alleged violations or "questionable activities" that the White House publicized in a report to Congress in January 1984.

Officially, Soviet diplomats naturally defended themselves against the charges of cheating, but unofficially other Soviets, who were authorized to discuss such matters, took a rather different line. As one of the *institutchiki* put it: "We hope the point is not lost on the Americans that by continuing to adhere to past agreements, despite the U.S.'s refusal to ratify them, we are accepting genuine restraints on our military capability, both in the offensive and defensive areas. And if the U.S. allows these agreements to lapse, we will, naturally, not be bound by those retraints. There are many things we can do." There seemed to be an unstated additional sentence: There are many things we are already beginning to do.

THE SOFTWARE CHALLENGE

In ideology and propaganda, as in arms control, Reagan turned out to be far worse, far more threatening than Carter had been in Soviet eyes.

Annoying and "inadmissible" as Carter's human rights campaign may have been when applied to the Soviets, it was also applied to Anastasio Somoza and Ferdinand Marcos. But Reagan's ideological advisers, particularly Jeane Kirkpatrick, designed a new typology claiming to distinguish between totalitarian and authoritarian regimes, with the obvious purpose of targeting the human rights campaign against the Soviet Union and its client states.

For all his tendency to scold and preach at the Soviets, Carter came into office with dreams—pipedreams, perhaps—of conciliation and disarmament. For all the trouble he had in getting to the summit, there was never any doubt that he wanted one. Reagan was quite another matter. Not only did he allow Soviet-American relations to deteriorate seriously (in doing that he had plenty of help from the Soviets themselves), but he also conveyed the impression, certainly during his first two years in office, that the relationship *ought* to be bad: the Soviets were such murderous, deceitful scoundrels that competition and confrontation were the only appropriate forms for the relationship; the Soviets did not deserve détente, by that or by any other name.

Unlike any of his predecessors, Reagan seemed not in the least tempted by summitry and agreements. Only in anticipation of his own re-election campaign, by late 1983, did Reagan finally decide that he wanted a summit after all, but that was almost solely because his political instincts and his political advisers told him that he needed one in order to command the high ground in the presidential election campaign.

Reagan seemed far less interested in meeting a Soviet leader at a summit than in seeing the Soviet system on the ash heap of history. He as much as said so in launching an ideological offensive against the U.S.S.R. under the banner of the "Democracy Campaign." According to a number of Soviet spokesmen, in their eyes Reagan crossed a certain threshold with a speech he delivered before the British Parliament on June 8, 1982.* Partly to please that particular audience but also to underscore the new themes in American foreign policy, Reagan quoted Winston Churchill repeatedly and echoed one of Churchill's most famous phrases, adjusting the original geographical coordinates of the Iron Curtain to take acocunt of Yugoslavia's independence. "From Stettin on the Baltic to Varna on the Black Sea," said Reagan, "the regimes planted by totalitarianism have had more than 30 years to establish their legitimacy." They had failed to do so. Reagan continued: "Any system is inherently unstable that has no peaceful means to legitimize its leaders." He talked about "the decay of the Soviet experiment," and a "great revolutionary crisis" within the Sovic bloc.

The bear-baiting continued in terms mockingly borrowed from the Communists themselves: "The march of freedom and democracy . . . will leave Marxism-Leninism on the ash heap of history as it has left other tyrannies which stifle the freedom and muzzle the self-expression of people." He talked of those "who strive and suffer for freedom within the confines of the Soviet Union itself," adding, "How we conduct ourselves here in the Western democracies will determine whether this trend continues . . . we must take actions to assist the campaign for democracy."

In an interview a few days after Reagan's appearance before Parliament, Leonid Zamyatin, an adviser to Brezhnev, took great umbrage at the speech, particularly at the word crusade. He kept coming back to it, saying that the President's use of the word "is a kind of turning point, a self-unmasking of American policy."

*See Appendix.

Reagan made quite clear, and his aides emphasized in their own amplifications of his speech, that he was not advocating military intervention or intimidation of the U.S.S.R.; he was proposing diplomatic pressure, through mechanisms such as the European Security Conference, and through such instruments of propaganda as the American-sponsored radio broadcasts to the U.S.S.R., which were under the control of conservatives marked by a particularly militant sense of their mission. While he was primarily calling for a crusade that would be peaceful and aboveboard, Reagan also had words of praise for "freedom-fighters" in countries with leftist regimes: Nicaragua, Ethiopia, Afghanistan, Cambodia, Angola, and Mozambique. There was also the supposedly covert side of the Democracy Campaign, but it was not all that covert, since some government officials openly boasted that the United States was taking the gloves off in the back alleys of the Third World, and the press was full of stories, leaked from the Administration as well as from the Congress, about the CIA's Directorate of Operations being back in business on a global scale.

Of even more concern to the Soviets were thinly veiled hints that the United States was looking for ways actively to encourage centrifugal forces inside Eastern Europe itself. Shortly after the imposition of martial law in Poland at the end of 1981, a Soviet diplomat was discussing the episode with an American counterpart. The Soviet invoked Franklin Roosevelt at Yalta, Harry Truman at Potsdam, Henry Kissinger in Helsinki and Helmut Sonnenfeldt in London as instances where the United States had acknowledged Eastern Europe as the Soviet sphere of influence. The American diplomat cut him off, saying, "Roosevelt and Truman are dead; Potsdam and Yalta are ancient history; Kissinger and Sonnenfeldt are private citizens. And even though you didn't mention it, we don't recognize the Brezhnev Doctrine either. It's a new ball game."*

All this sounded to Soviet ears very much like the revival of the thirty-five-year-old notion of "rollback" (a phrase used by John Foster Dulles, among others, to mean driving the Soviets out of Eastern Europe). A high official of the United States Information Agency, Scott Thompson, gave a series of supposedly off-the-record lectures, some of them to audiences of U.S. military officers, saying that the world had moved into the "post-containment era," and it was time to "take the struggle directly to the enemy, on his own ground." He was talking about the ideological struggle, not a military one. But when word of his remarks found its way into the Washington rumor mill and from there to the Soviet embassy in Washington, it contributed to the impression that the U.S.S.R. was dealing with a new phenomenon—an Administration that seemed truly and unprecedentedly committed to the goal of doing the Soviet Union in.

*In 1976, Sonnenfeldt, who was then the Counselor of the State Department under Henry Kissinger, gave a speech to a closed-door meeting of American ambassadors in which he spoke of an "organic" relationship between the U.S.S.R. and its satellites. When a somewhat distorted version of his remarks, including that one phrase, leaked in the press, Sonnenfeldt was pilloried by conservative columnists and congressmen for allegedly accepting and even endorsing Soviet hegemony over Eastern Europe. This version of what he had said was dubbed the Sonnenfeldt Doctrine (although not by Sonnenfeldt himself). The Brezhnev Doctrine was the Soviet claim, in the wake of the invasion of Czechoslovakia in 1968, that the U.S.S.R. had the right to protect "the gains of socialism" in any "fraternal" country where they were in jeopardy.

There was a theme in the Reagan rhetoric, especially in the first two years, that went beyond condemnation and suggested not only that the United States would like to be in on the execution, but that the Soviet system might be rolled back right to the gates of the Kremlin itself. The suggestion that the United States had an opportunity and even an obligation to help the U.S.S.R. on its way to the ash heap of history was sometimes proposed optimistically, as when Ronald Reagan assured the graduating class of the University of Notre Dame in 1981 that "the West won't contain Communism, it will transcend Communism. It won't bother to denounce it; it will dismiss it as some bizarre chapter in human history whose last pages are even now being written." Sometimes this idea was couched in terms of alarm, when he denounced Soviet Communism with great frequency and vehemence, portraying the U.S.S.R. as a mortal danger to the very survival of the West, a danger that must be actively opposed and ultimately defeated.

Some members of the Administration persisted in an unprecedented assertion that the United States had the ability to effect crucial changes at the very core, and at the very top, of the Soviet system. The Reagan Administration believed, for a long time, that it could influence the composition and orientation of the post-Brezhnev leadership. It felt it had an opportunity to play Kremlin politics, and it had a theory for beating the system, of using an American hard line to enhance the competitive position of softliners against hardliners who were vying for power in the post-Brezhnev era.

Speaking privately, other Administration officials, especially professional diplomats and intelligence analysts with long experience in Soviet affairs, not only disavowed the notion that the United States could manipulate Soviet internal politics, but they expressed confidence that the Soviets recognized such theorizing for what it was: idiosyncratic, extremist and very much confined to the fringes of the government.

The principal theoretician of the view that the Soviet system could be tamed if not dismantled was Richard Pipes, a scholar of Russian history, who served as senior Kremlinologist for the National Security Council staff during the Administration's first two years. Soviet officials were perfectly prepared to agree that Pipes was an extremist; they noted with undisguised relief his return to Harvard and his eventual replacement at the NSC by a career Foreign Service officer, Jack Matlock. But they were not ready to treat Pipes and his theories as an aberration. They noted that his controversial view about the vulnerability of the internal workings of the Soviet Union to external manipulation found echoes in speeches by Alexander Haig, Richard Allen, William Clark and the President himself. Even after Haig and Allen left the government and Clark eventually moved from being National Security Adviser to Secretary of the Interior, Soviets continued to cite their statements as expressions of the spirit of the Administration.

In their view, the Administration continued to harbor individuals they considered to be pathological (or, in the Russian term, "zoological") enemies, people dedicated to the eventual defeat of the U.S.S.R. The person cited most often in this connection has been Richard Perle, the Assistant Secretary of Defense for International Security Affairs. Despite his second-echelon post, Perle has indeed been extraordinarily influential, particularly in arms-control policy. Before joining the Administration, he worked for many years as the right hand man to the late Senator Henry Jackson, Democrat of Washington, the leading critic of détente and the Soviets' least favorite American political figure before Reagan came along.

Early in the Administration, two others were also cited as foxes who had been allowed into the chicken coop of Soviet-American relations: Eugene Rostow, the director of the Arms Control and Disarmament Agency, and Paul Nitze. But Rostow was driven out of the Administration, partly (though by no means solely) because he favored a more accommodating policy in the Intermediate-range Nuclear Forces talks, and Nitze ended up being the in-house moderate, stymied in his efforts to achieve a breakthrough in INF by Administration hardliners, notably including Perle.

"What are we to make of an Administration," asked Georgi Arbatov, "in which the founders of the Committee on the Present Danger [Rostow and Nitze] are relative doves?"*

It is tempting for an American to dismiss Soviet grievances by saying it serves them right; they can dish it out but they can't take it. For decades, Americans have listened to Soviet leaders talk about how their system would bury ours and how the ideological struggle must continue even in periods of peaceful coexistence between states and friendly relations between peoples.

*The Committee on the Present Danger was a bipartisan, private group that campaigned against SALT II and in favor of higher defense spending. A number of its more prominent members joined the Reagan Administration.

In 1983, the Soviet press portrayed Reagan as a new Hitler. Arbatov's Institute for the Study of the U.S.A. and Canada has devoted considerable energy to grinding out what it calls "counterpropaganda," depicting American policy and policymakers in the most lurid and ludicrous terms. Leonid Zamyatin's International Information Department of the Central Committee exists largely to wage political warfare against the West.

What was Reagan doing but giving the Soviets a dose of their own medicine? The U.S. policy of containment, or even post-containment, was nothing but a response to a Soviet policy of expansion. Besides, sticks and stones might break their bones, but why should the Soviets take mere words so hurtfully? Since when had they become so thin-skinned?

These questions are fair enough if one is interested in puncturing the self-righteousness that Soviet spokesmen exude in those sterile, frustrating arguments that so often dominate encounters between Soviets and Westerners. But if one's purpose is to understand the debates that probably go on among Soviets themselves, the obvious and justified rebuttals to Zamyatin and others are beside the point. What matters is that the Soviets are, in their peculiar way, very thin-skinned indeed; and certain words, particularly those with which they have been abused by the Reagan Administration, particularly during a time of troubles in Poland, are very like real sticks and stones.

As Ambassador Dobrynin said in his remarks at the none-too-cheerful celebration in Washington in November of the fiftieth anniversary of diplomatic relations, "For us, words are deeds."

SOFT PROBES, HARD BLOWS

There is reason to suspect that the impact of the American hard line on those internal Soviet debates and on evolution of the leadership may have been just the opposite from the one intended. The effect may have been to strengthen those men in the Politburo, the Central Committee, and the security apparatus who had been pressing a mirror-image of Reagan's own thesis: perhaps the relationship may indeed be inherently, permanently, and predeterminedly bad.

While there still seems to be no debate in the U.S.S.R. over whether détente was a good thing, and certainly no debate over whose fault it was that it failed, there may well have been a heated dispute over whether détente has failed forever. Is grinding hostility the norm in the relationship, and was détente an aberration? Or was détente the norm, and is the Reagan's anti-Sovietism an aberration? If the first view prevails—that détente is dead—then that would lead to a policy of protracted military buildup, preparing for a long siege, and, no doubt, of countermeasures on a variety of fronts. If the other view prevails—that détente is only dormant—that would suggest patience, more tentative military measures, adopting an attitude of suffering through the Reagan Administration until a more congenial American leadership arrives on the scene.

The Americanologists, who had a vested interest in the resumption of détente, tended early on to talk about the "immutable realities" underlying détente and to quote Brezhnev's line about the "irreversibility" of the process. Valentin Zorin liked to point out that slogans and labels for policies might change, but "it is beyond any doubt that the American leaders will go back to realities which, at the beginning of the '70s, forced a rather conservative politician, such as President Nixon, to admit that Washington must 'make a painful re-evaluation' of its policy." Even Chernenko, the man destined to succeed Andropov, had vowed that if "Washington proves unable to rise above primitive anti-Communism," the U.S.S.R. will simply wait it out: "We believe in reason and we believe that sooner or later—and the sooner the better—reason will triumph." Andropov himself, in a speech to the November 1982 Central Committee plenum, said, "We are convinced that the '70s, characterized by détente, were not . . . a chance episode in the difficult history of mankind. No, the policy of détente is by no means a past stage. . . ."

What these spokesmen had in mind when they talked about "reality" was the military strength of the Soviet Union, its irreversible achievement of equality with the United States. What they mean by "reason" is the American acknowledgment of that strength and that irreversibility.

Through mid-1983, there were some interesting but inconclusive signs that the deterioration might indeed have bottomed out. The many factors that had led the Soviets to want a *peredyshka*, or breathing space, in 1981 were still there. Now instead of an old and ailing Brezhnev, it was an old and ailing Andropov in charge. The U.S.S.R. still had good reason to think long and hard about its vulnerabilities at home, within the Eastern bloc, in Europe, and in the Third World. Systemic weakness and international overextension were, if anything, bigger problems than ever. The American leadership, anticipating the election, was clearly beginning to think about the desirability of a summit and an arms control agreement in 1984. U.S. and Soviet diplomats were holding tentative discussions at a variety of levels, probing each other on what it might take to re-establish a *modus vivendi* on geopolitical as well as bilateral issues.

Then came the Korean airliner affair, Reagan's bitter denunciation at the United Nations, and Andropov's retaliatory blow a few days later. Many American officials and some outside experts as well were convinced that had it not been for the tragedy of Flight 007, there might have been a major breakthrough in late 1983 or early 1984—in time to do Reagan the most good politically. Some thought that the harm done by the Korean airliner incident would turn out to have been brief, and that there would still be a breakthrough of some kind in 1984.

Perhaps, but there is ample room for skepticism. For one thing, if substantive, albeit incipient progress had been achieved behind the scenes in early and mid-1983, it is puzzling why the downing of the airplane should have stopped it. Outrageous as the incident was, it was a fluke; the plane was not American, and it was indisputably off course, over Soviet territory. The negative consequences of the affair for Soviet-American relations seemed disproportionate—unless, of course, it crystalized negative trends that were already far advanced.

If the Soviet leaders were looking for a *modus vivendi* with the United States—and if they believed that the Reagan Administration was also interested in such a thing—why would the Politburo, speaking through its ailing chief on September 28, have let the Korean airliner incident prompt a drastic shift in course, or the abandonment of a new policy? The answer may be that the September 28 statement did not represent a shift or an abandonment; rather, it may have ratified a policy that had been gathering momentum for some time.

Even if that was the case, then the question still lingers why the Korean airliner affair should have prompted such an outburst—a premeditated, consensus-approved, committee-drafted outburst—of door-slamming, bridge-burning rhetoric. The answer there may be that the American response to the downing of the plane served to confirm that the U.S. leadership was simply out to get the Soviet Union and deprive it of its legitimacy as a member of the world community, not to mention as a co-equal superpower.

The most important, and certainly the most quoted, sentence in Andropov's statement was: "Even if someone had any illusions about the possible evolution for the better in the policy of the present U.S. Administration, the latest developments have finally dispelled them." The key word was "finally." That adverb seemed to suggest that a final determination had been made, that the debate was over.*

*Some sources in Moscow believed to be associated with Andropov's old stomping ground, the KGB, put the story around that the "no-illusions" passage was actually self-critical; Andropov himself had been the only one still nurturing such illusions. Foreign Ministry officials, meanwhile urged readers to pay closer attention to the end of the statement, where Andropov was quoted as saying that despite all that had gone before, the U.S.S.R. would continue the search for peace. It was, as the Soviets like to say, no accident that West Europeans were particularly urged to read the statement in this way.

Of course, nothing is ever really final—in words or deeds, in attitudes or actions—unless the finality is sealed with thermonuclear explosions. And those, at least, seemed no closer to going off after Andropov's statement than before. For all the political poison in the air, the two countries continued to behave with the greatest caution in any situation that might have led to military conflict. The Soviets cannot, as a practical matter, unilaterally declare their dealings with the United States at an end. Neither the U.S. National Security Council not the Politburo can make the other disappear with high-level pronouncements or by any other means.

All that is as true as it is reassuring. What is not so certain is whether Andropov's statement of September 28 will sound as faint in mid-1984 as Reagan's March 8 comments on "the focus of evil." So the Administration hopes. Reagan at the end of 1983 said he had no plans to make any more "Darth Vader" speeches and tried to set an example for a new, less polemical tone in his speech on January 16, although he pointedly refused to repudiate his earlier harsh words ("We don't refuse to talk when the Soviets call us imperialist aggressors and worse or because they cling to the fantasy of a Communist triumph over democracy"). The implication was that the Soviet leaders, too, should do their share to change the tone and substance of the relationship in the new year. Many of Reagan's aides and defenders pointed out that regardless of how serious and promising the mutual probes had been in early 1983, self-interest on both sides would suggest further such probes in 1984.

The disagreement between distinguished American experts on this score was neatly summed up in the following exchange: Dimitri Simes judged that the Soviet leaders had adopted a posture of "strategic pessimism and tactical flexibility"—that is, battening down for a long period of confrontation and tension with the United States, while maneuvering for political and propaganda advantages, particularly with the West Europeans.

Helmut Sonnenfeldt disagreed; he saw the Soviets preserving their "strategic flexibility" while voicing "tactical pessimism." In other words, they were prepared to do business with the Reagan Administration at any time that it suited their purposes and interests, Andropov to the contrary notwithstanding, and Soviet proclamations of gloom and doom like Andropov's are nothing more than pressure tactics, or scare tactics, to get the United States to do business all the sooner and all the more on Soviet terms.

Strategic and tactical have always been somewhat arbitrary terms. There is a third possibility: that the Andropov line of September 28 will hold for what might be called the intermediate-range future—through the American presidential elections. What is known about the nature and behavior of the Soviet leadership, coupled with what evidence we have about current attitudes—evidence derived from both words and deeds—suggests that the Soviets may be settling in for a siege of at least that duration.

Andropov's death in February 1984 was seen by some in the Administration as an opportunity to end the siege mentality—or at least to get credit on the home front and in Europe for trying. President Reagan and Secretary of State Shultz were extraordinarily conciliatory in their public comments on Andropov's passing and Chernenko's accession to the leadership of the

Party. In reply, the Soviets seemed willing to strike a few conciliatory notes of their own, if only to prevent the Americans from outflanking them rhetorically.

However, these were very much the same Soviet leaders who had been making judgments and communicating to the world through Andropov's disembodied statements and *Pravda* "interviews" during the long months of his infirmity. His September 28 statement had spoken for them: it had put them on record, at the highest level, for the first time, in the most emphatic terms, as having given up on trying to do business with an American Administration—the same Administration that was now making soothing noises.

The Politburo members had presumably been maneuvering for their places in the post-Andropov order for a long time, back during the chilly fall of 1983 before the spring thaw of 1984. That meant they had, very likely, already staked out their positions before the moderation in tone by Washington. In their obsession with continuity, the last thing they would probably want to convey was any impression that the death of one of their own number might be accompanied by some sort of shakeup in attitudes or personnel that their adversaries could exploit. Besides, they understood well enough the Administration's political motivations for softening its talk. Questions surely persisted about whether the Administration was now, by Soviet definition, "serious." The putative emergence of a new Reagan in 1984 proved nothing to the men in the Kremlin except that he seriously wanted to be re-elected. If, contrary to their initial suspicions, it turned out that there had indeed been a basic and enduring shift in American policy, that would become apparent only after the election, and even then only after some time had passed. Even if the Administration did begin to budge on the substance of its positions, there would be a strong inclination in Moscow to see how much further the Americans would come before reciprocal Soviet concessions were necessary. That process, too, would take time, especially since it would coincide both with the campaign in the United States and a period of transition and consolidation in the Kremlin.

APPENDICES

Ronald Reagan
Address to Members of Parliament
June 8, 1982

My Lord Chancellor, Mr. Speaker:

The journey of which this visit forms a part is a long one. Already it has taken me to two great cities of the West, Rome and Paris, and to the economic summit at Versailles. And there, once again, our sister democracies have proved that even in a time of severe economic strain, free peoples can work together freely and voluntarily to address problems as serious as inflation, unemployment, trade, and economic development in a spirit of cooperation and solidarity.

Other milestones lie ahead. Later this week, in Germany, we and our NATO allies will discuss measures for our joint defense and America's latest initiatives for a more peaceful, secure world through arms reductions.

Each stop of this trip is important, but among them all, this moment occupies a special place in my heart and in the hearts of my countrymen—a moment of kinship and homecoming in these hallowed halls.

Speaking for all Americans, I want to say how very much at home we feel in your house. Every American would, because this is, as we have been so eloquently told, one of democracy's shrines. Here the rights of free people and the processes of representation have been debated and refined.

It has been said that an institution is the lengthening shadow of a man. This institution is the lengthening shadow of all the men and and women who have sat here and all those who have voted to send representatives here.

This is my second visit to Great Britain as President of the United States. My first opportunity to stand on British soil occurred almost a year and a half ago when your Prime Minister graciously hosted a diplomatic dinner at the British Embassy in Washington. Mrs. Thatcher said then that she hoped I was not distressed to find staring down at me from the grand staircase a portrait of His Royal Majesty King George III. She suggested it was best to let bygones be bygones, and in view of our two countries' remarkable friendship in succeeding years, she added that most Englishmen today would agree with Thomas Jefferson that "a little rebellion now and then is a very good thing."

Well, from here I will go to Bonn and then Berlin, where there stands a grim symbol of power untamed. The Berlin Wall, that dreadful gray gash across the city, is in its third decade. It is the fitting signature of the regime that built it.

And a few hundred kilometers behind the Berlin Wall, there is another symbol. In the center of Warsaw, there is a sign that notes the distances to two capitals. In one direction it points toward Moscow. In the other it points toward Brussels, headquarters of Western Europe's tangible unity. The marker says that the distances from Warsaw to Moscow and Warsaw to Brussels are equal. The sign makes this point: Poland is not East or West. Poland is at the center of European civilization. It has contributed mightily to that civilization. It is doing so today by being magnificently unreconciled to oppression.

Poland's struggle to be Poland and to secure the basic rights we often take for granted demonstrates why we dare not take those rights for granted. Gladstone, defending the Reform Bill of 1866, declared, "You cannot fight against the future. Time is on our side." It was easier to believe in the march of democracy in Gladstone's day—in that high noon of Victorian optimism.

We're approaching the end of a bloody century plagued by a terrible political invention—totalitarianism. Optimism comes less easily today, not because democracy is less vigorous, but because democracy's enemies have refined their instruments of repression. Yet optimism is in order, because day by day democracy is proving itself to be a not-at-all-fragile flower. From Stettin on the Baltic to Varna on the Black Sea, the regimes planted by totalitarianism have had more than 30 years to establish their legitimacy. But none—not one regime—has yet been able to risk free elections. Regimes planted by bayonets do not take root.

The strength of the Solidarity movement in Poland demonstrates the truth told in an underground joke in the Soviet Union. It is that the Soviet Union would remain a one-party nation even if an opposition party were permitted, because everyone would join the opposition party.

America's time as a player on the stage of world history has been brief. I think understanding this fact has always made you patient with your younger cousins—well, not always patient. I do recall that on one occasion, Sir Winston Churchill said in exasperation about one of our most distinguished diplomats: "He is the only case I know of a bull who carries his china shop with him."

But witty as Sir Winston was, he also had that special attribute of great statesmen—the gift of vision, the willingness to see the future based on the experience of the past. It is this sense of history, this understanding of the past that I want to talk with you about today, for it is in remembering what we share of the past that our two nations can make common cause for the future.

We have not inherited an easy world. If developments like the Industrial Revolution, which began here in England, and the gifts of science and technology have made life much easier for us, they have also made it more dangerous. There are threats now to our freedom, indeed to our very existence, that other generations could never even have imagined.

There is first the threat of global war. No President, no Congress, no Prime Minister, no Parliament can spend a day entirely free of this threat. And I don't have to tell you that in today's world the existence of nuclear weapons could mean, if not the extinction of mankind, then surely the end of civilization as we know it. That's why negotiations on intermediate-range nuclear forces now underway in Europe and the START talks—Strategic Arms Reduction Talks—which will begin later this month, are not just critical to American or Western policy; they are critical to mankind. Our commitment to early success in these negotiations is firm and unshakable, and our purpose is clear: reducing the risk of war by reducing the means of waging war on both sides.

At the same time there is a threat posed to human freedom by the enormous power of the modern state. History teaches the dangers of government that overreaches—political control taking precedence over free economic growth, secret police, mindless bureaucracy, all combining to stifle individual excellence and personal freedom.

Now, I'm aware that among us here and throughout Europe there is legitimate disagreement over the extent to which the public sector should play a role in a nation's economy and life. But on one point all of us are united—our abhorrence of dictatorship in all its forms, but most particularly totalitarianism and the terrible inhumanities it has caused in our time—the great purge, Auschwitz and Dachau, the Gulag, and Cambodia.

Historians looking back at our time will note the consistent restraint and peaceful intentions of the West. They will note that it was the democracies who refused to use the threat of their nuclear monopoly in the forties and early fifties for territorial or imperial gain. Had that nuclear monopoly been in the hands of the Communist world, the map of Europe—indeed, the world—would look very different today. And certainly they will note it was not the democracies that invaded Afghanistan or suppressed Polish Solidarity or used chemical and toxin warfare in Afghanistan and Southeast Asia.

If history teaches anything it teaches self-delusion in the face of unpleasant facts is folly. We see around us today the marks of our terrible dilemma—predictions of doomsday, antinuclear demonstrations, an arms race in which the West must, for its own protection, be an unwilling participant. At the same time we see totalitarian forces in the world who seek subversion and conflict around the globe to further their barbarous assault on the human spirit. What, then, is our course? Must civilization perish in a hail of fiery atoms? Must freedom wither in a quiet, deadening accommodation with totalitarian evil?

Sir Winston Churchill refused to accept the inevitability of war or even that it was imminent. He said, "I do not believe that Soviet Russia desires war. What they desire is the fruits of war and the indefinite expansion of their power and doctrines. But what we have to consider here today while time remains is the permanent prevention of war and the establishment of conditions of freedom and democracy as rapidly as possible in all countries."

Well, this is precisely our mission today: to preserve freedom as well as peace. It may not be easy to see; but I believe we live now at a turning point.

In an ironic sense Karl Marx was right. We are witnessing today a great revolutionary crisis, a crisis where the demands of the economic order are conflicting directly with those of the political order. But the crisis is happening not in the free, non-Marxist West, but in the home of Marxist-Leninism, the Soviet Union. It is the Soviet Union that runs against the tide of history by denying human freedom and human dignity to its citizens. It also is in deep economic difficulty. The rate of growth in the national product has been steadily declining since the fifties and is less than half of what it was then.

The dimensions of this failure are astounding: A country which employs one-fifth of its population in agriculture is unable to feed its own people. Were it not for the private sector, the tiny private sector tolerated in Soviet agriculture, the country might be on the brink of famine. These private plots occupy a bare 3 percent of the arable land but account for nearly one-quarter of Soviet farm output and nearly one-third of meat products and vegetables. Overcentralized, with little or no incentives, year after year the Soviet system

storming
War II.
same hum
Central A
news med
after day
toward th
governme
ple of that
 And th
offered a
ment they
the hills
ban-back
and their
threatene
dreds of b
ting to the
ple of El
them, bra
miles to v
 They s
turn to vo
as observe
rifle fire
the line to
voted. A
rillas she
polls, and
can kill m
us all." T
out to be
old, the i

Strange, but in my own country there's been little if any news coverage of that war since the election. Now, perhaps they'll say it's—well, because there are newer struggles now.

On distant islands in the South Atlantic young men are fighting for Britain. And, yes, voices have been raised protesting their sacrifice for lumps of rock and earth so far away. But those young men aren't fighting for mere real estate. They fight for a cause—for the belief that armed aggression must not be allowed to succeed, and the people must participate in the decisions of government—the decisions of government under the rule of law. If there had been firmer support for that principle some 45 years ago, perhaps our generation wouldn't have suffered the bloodletting of World War II.

In the Middle East now the guns sound once more, this time in Lebanon, a country that for too long has had to endure the tragedy of civil war, terrorism, and foreign intervention and occupation. The fighting in Lebanon on the part of all parties must stop, and Israel should bring its forces home. But this is not enough. We must all work to stamp out the scourge of terrorism that in the Middle East makes war an ever-present threat.

But beyond the troublespots lies a deeper, more positive pattern. Around the world today, the democratic revolution is gathering new strength. In India a critical test has been passed with the peaceful change of governing political parties. In Africa, Nigeria is moving into remarkable and unmistakable ways to build and strengthen its democratic institutions. In the Caribbean and Central America, 16 of 24 countries have freely elected governments. And in the United Nations, 8 of the 10 developing nations which have joined that body in the past 5 years are democracies.

In the Communist world as well, man's instinctive desire for freedom and self-determination surfaces again and again. To be sure, there are grim reminders of how brutally the police state attempts to snuff out this quest for self-rule—1953 in East Germany, 1956 in Hungary, 1968 in Czechoslovakia, 1981 in Poland. But the struggle continues in Poland. And we know that there are even those who strive and suffer for freedom within the confines of the Soviet Union itself. How we conduct ourselves here in the Western democracies will determine whether this trend continues.

No, democracy is not a fragile flower. Still it needs cultivating. If the rest of this century is to witness the gradual growth of freedom and democratic ideals, we must take actions to assist the campaign for democracy.

Some argue that we should encourage democratic change in right-wing dictatorships, but not in Communist regimes. Well, to accept this preposterous notion—as some well-meaning people have—is to invite the argument that once countries achieve a nuclear capability, they should be allowed an undisturbed reign of terror over their own citizens. We reject this course.

As for the Soviet view, Chairman Brezhnev repeatedly has stressed that the competition of ideas and systems must continue and that this is entirely consistent with relaxation of tensions and peace.

Well, we ask only that these systems begin by living up to their own constitutions, abiding by their own laws, and complying with the international obligations they have undertaken. We ask only for a process, a direction, a basic code of decency, not for an instant transformation.

We cannot ignore the fact that even without our encouragement there has been and will continue to be repeated explosions against repression and dictatorships. The Soviet Union itself is not immune to this reality. Any system is inherently unstable that has no peaceful means to legitimize its leaders. In such cases, the very repressiveness of the state ultimately drives people to resist it, if necessary, by force.

While we must be cautious about forcing the pace of change, we must not hesitate to declare our ultimate objectives and to take concrete actions to move toward them. We must be staunch in our conviction that freedom is not the sole prerogative of a lucky few, but the inalienable and universal right of all human beings. So states the United Nations Universal Declaration of Human Rights, which, among other things, guarantees free elections.

The objective I propose is quite simple to state: to foster the infrastructure of democracy, the system of a free press, unions, political parties, universities, which allows a people to choose their own way to develop their own culture, to reconcile their own differences through peaceful means.

This is not cultural imperialism, it is providing the means for genuine self-determination and protection for diversity. Democracy already flourishes in countries with very different cultures and historical experiences. It would be cultural condescension, or worse, to say that any people prefer dictatorship to democracy. Who would voluntarily choose not to have the right to vote, decide to purchase government propaganda handouts instead of independent newspapers, prefer government to worker-controlled unions, opt for land to be owned by the state instead of those who till it, want government repression of religious liberty, a single political party instead of a free choice, a rigid cultural orthodoxy instead of democratic tolerance and diversity?

Since 1917 the Soviet Union has given covert political training and assistance to Marxist-Leninists in many countries. Of course, it also has promoted the use of violence and subversion by these same forces. Over the past several decades, West European and other Social Democrats, Christian Democrats, and leaders have offered open assistance to fraternal, political, and social institutions to bring about peaceful and democratic progress. Appropriately, for a vigorous new democracy, the Federal Republic of Germany's political foundations have become a major force in this effort.

We in America now intend to take additional steps, as many of our allies have already done, toward realizing this same goal. The chairmen and other leaders of the national Republican and Democratic Party organizations are initiating a study with the bipartisan American political foundation to determine how the United States can best contribute as a nation to the global campaign for democracy now gathering force. They will have the cooperation of congressional leaders of both parties, along with representatives of business, labor, and other major institutions in our society. I look forward to receiving their recommendations and to working with these institutions and the Congress in the common task of strengthening democracy throughout the world.

It is time that we committed ourselves as a nation—

in both the public and private sectors—to assisting democratic development.

We plan to consult with leaders of other nations as well. There is a proposal before the Council of Europe to invite parliamentarians from democratic countries to a meeting next year in Strasbourg. That prestigious gathering could consider ways to help democratic political movements.

This November in Washington there will take place an international meeting on free elections. And next spring there will be a conference of world authorities on constitutionalism and self-government hosted by the Chief Justice of the United States. Authorities from a number of developing and developed countries—judges, philosophers, and politicians with practical experience—have agreed to explore how to turn principle into practice and further the rule of law.

At the same time, we invite the Soviet Union to consider with us how the competition of ideas and values—which it is committed to support—can be conducted on a peaceful and reciprocal basis. For example, I am prepared to offer President Brezhnev an opportunity to speak to the American people on our television if he will allow me the same opportunity with the Soviet people. We also suggest that panels of our newsmen periodically appear on each other's television to discuss major events.

Now, I don't wish to sound overly optimistic, yet the Soviet Union is not immune from the reality of what is going on in the world. It has happened in the past—a small ruling elite either mistakenly attempts to ease domestic unrest through greater repression and foreign adventure, or it chooses a wiser course. It begins to allow its people a voice in their own destiny. Even if this latter process is not realized soon, I believe the renewed strength of the democratic movement, complemented by a global campaign for freedom, will strengthen the prospects for arms control and a world at peace.

I have discussed on other occasions, including my address on May 9th, the elements of Western policies toward the Soviet Union to safeguard our interests and protect the peace. What I am describing now is a plan and a hope for the long term—the march of freedom and democracy which will leave Marxism-Leninism on the ashheap of history as it has left other tyrannies which stifle the freedom and muzzle the self-expression of the people. And that's why we must continue our efforts to strengthen NATO even as we move forward with our Zero-Option initiative in the negotiations on intermediate-range forces and our proposal for a one-third reduction in strategic ballistic missile warheads.

Our military strength is a prerequisite to peace, but let it be clear we maintain this strength in the hope it will never be used, for the ultimate determinant in the struggle that's now going on in the world will not be bombs and rockets, but a test of wills and ideas, a trial of spiritual resolve, the values we hold, the beliefs we cherish, the ideals to which we are dedicated.

The British people know that, given strong leadership, time and a little bit of hope, the forces of good ultimately rally and triumph over evil. Here among you is the cradle of self-government, the Mother of Parliaments. Here is the enduring greatness of the British contribution to mankind, the great civilized ideas: individual liberty, representative government, and the rule of law under God.

I've often wondered about the shyness of some of us in the West about standing for these ideals that have done so much to ease the plight of man and the hardships of our imperfect world. This reluctance to use those vast resources at our command reminds me of the elderly lady whose home was bombed in the Blitz. As the rescuers moved about, they found a bottle of brandy she'd stored behind the staircase, which was all that was left standing. And since she was barely conscious, one of the workers pulled the cork to give her a taste of it. She came around immediately and said, "Here now—there now, put it back. That's for emergencies."

Well, the emergency is upon us. Let us be shy no longer. Let us go to our strength. Let us offer hope. Let us tell the world that a new age is not only possible but probable.

During the dark days of the Second World War, when this island was incandescent with courage, Winston Churchill exclaimed about Britain's adversaries, "What kind of a people do they think we are?" Well, Britain's adversaries found out what extraordinary people the British are. But all the democracies paid a terrible price for allowing the dictators to underestimate us. We dare not make that mistake again. So, let us ask ourselves, "What kind of people do we think we are?" And let us answer, "Free people, worthy of freedom and determined not only to remain so but to help others gain their freedom as well."

Sir Winston led his people to great victory in war and then lost an election just as the fruits of victory were about to be enjoyed. But he left office honorably, and, as it turned out, temporarily, knowing that the liberty of his people was more important than the fate of any single leader. History recalls his greatness in ways no dictator will ever know. And he left us a message of hope for the future, as timely now as when he first uttered it, as opposition leader in the Commons nearly 27 years ago, when he said, "When we look back on all the perils through which we have passed and at the mighty foes that we have laid low and all the dark and deadly designs that we have frustrated, why should we fear for our future? We have," he said, "come safely through the worst."

Well, the task I've set forth will long outlive our own generation. But together, we too have come through the worst. Let us now begin a major effort to secure the best—a crusade for freedom that will engage the faith and fortitude of the next generation. For the sake of peace and justice, let us move toward a world in which all people are at last free to determine their own destiny.

Thank you.

Ronald Reagan

Remarks to the National Association of Evangelicals

March 8, 1983

Delivered at the Annual Convention in Orlando, Florida

Reverend clergy all, Senator Hawkins, distinguished members of the Florida congressional delegation, and all of you:

I can't tell you how you have warmed my heart with your welcome. I'm delighted to be here today.

Those of you in the National Association of Evangelicals are known for your spiritual and humanitarian work. And I would be especially remiss if I didn't discharge right now one personal debt of gratitude. Thank you for your prayers. Nancy and I have felt their presence many times in many ways. And believe me, for us they've made all the difference.

The other day in the East Room of the White House at a meeting there, someone asked me whether I was aware of all the people out there who were praying for the President. And I had to say, "Yes, I am. I've felt it. I believe in intercessionary prayer." But I couldn't help but say to that questioner after he'd asked the question that—or at least say to them that if sometimes when he was praying he got a busy signal, it was just me in there ahead of him. I think I understand how Abraham Lincoln felt when he said, "I have been driven many times to my knees by the overwhelming conviction that I had nowhere else to go."

From the joy and the good feeling of this conference, I go to a political reception. Now, I don't know why, but that bit of scheduling reminds me of a story which I'll share with you.

An evangelical minister and a politician arrived at Heaven's gate one day together. And St. Peter, after doing all the necessary formalities, took them in hand to show them where their quarters would be. And he took them to a small, single room with a bed, a chair, and a table and said this was for the clergyman. And the politician was a little worried about what might be in store for him. And he couldn't believe it then when St. Peter stopped in front of a beautiful mansion with lovely grounds, many servants, and told him that these would be his quarters.

And he couldn't help but ask, he said, "But wait, how—there's something wrong—how do I get this mansion while that good and holy man only gets a single room?" And St. Peter said, "You have to understand how things are up here. We've got thousands and thousands of clergy. You're the first politician who ever made it."

But I don't want to contribute to a stereotype. So, I tell you there are a great many God-fearing, dedicated, noble men and women in public life, present company included. And, yes, we need your help to keep us ever mindful of the ideas and the principles that brought us into the public arena in the first place. The basis of those ideals and principles is a commitment to freedom and personal liberty that, itself, is grounded in the much deeper realization that freedom prospers only where the blessings of God are avidly sought and humbly accepted.

The American experiment in democracy rests on this insight. Its discovery was the great triumph of our Founding Fathers, voiced by William Penn when he said: "If we will not be governed by God, we must be governed by tyrants." Explaining the inalienable rights of men, Jefferson said, "The God who gave us life, gave us liberty at the same time." And it was George Washington who said that "of all the dispositions and habits which lead to political prosperity, religion and morality are indispensable supports."

And finally, that shrewdest of all observers of American democracy, Alexis de Tocqueville, put it eloquently after he had gone on a search for the secret of America's greatness and genius—and he said: "Not until I went into the churches of America and heard her pulpits aflame with righteousness did I understand the greatness and the genius of America. . . . America is good. And if America ever ceases to be good, America will cease to be great."

Well, I'm pleased to be here today with you who are keeping America great by keeping her good. Only through your work and prayers and those of millions of others can we hope to survive this perilous century and keep alive this experiment in liberty, this last, best hope of man.

I want you to know that this administration is motivated by a political philosophy that sees the greatness of America in you, her people, and in your families, churches, neighborhoods, communities—the institutions that foster and nourish values like concern for others and respect for the rule of law under God.

Now, I don't have to tell you that this puts us in opposition to, or at least out of step with, a prevailing attitude of many who have turned to a modern-day secularism, discarding the tried and time-tested values upon which our very civilization is based. No matter how well intentioned, their value system is radically different from that of most Americans. And while they proclaim that they're freeing us from superstitions of the past, they've taken upon themselves the job of superintending us by government rule and regulation. Sometimes their voices are louder than ours, but they are not yet a majority.

An example of that vocal superiority is evident in a controversy now going on in Washington. And since I'm involved, I've been waiting to hear from the parents of young America. How far are they willing to go in giving to government their prerogatives as parents?

Let me state the case as briefly and simply as I can. An organization of citizens, sincerely motivated and deeply concerned about the increase in illegitimate births and abortions involving girls well below the age of consent, sometime ago established a nationwide network of clinics to offer help to these girls and, hopefully, alleviate this situation. Now, again, let me say, I do not fault their intent. However, in their well-intentioned effort, these clinics have decided to provide advice and birth control drugs and devices to underage girls without the knowledge of their parents.

For some years now, the Federal Government has helped with funds to subsidize these clinics. In providing for this, the Congress decreed that every effort would be made to maximize parental participation. Nevertheless, the drugs and devices are prescribed without getting parental consent or giving notification after they've done so. Girls termed "sexually active"—and that has replaced the word "promiscuous"—are given this help in order to prevent illegitimate birth or abortion.

Well, we have ordered clinics receiving Federal funds to notify the parents such help has been given. One of the Nation's leading newspapers has created the term "squeal rule" in editorializing against us for doing this, and we're being criticized for violating the privacy of young people. A judge has recently granted an injunction against an enforcement of our rule. I've watched TV panel shows discuss this issue, seen columnists pontificating on our error, but no one seems to mention morality as playing a part in the subject of sex.

Is all of Judeo-Christian tradition wrong? Are we to believe that something so sacred can be looked upon as a purely physical thing with no potential for emotional and psychological harm? And isn't it the parents' right to give counsel and advice to keep their children from making mistakes that may affect their entire lives?

Many of us in government would like to know what parents think about this intrusion in their family by government. We're going to fight in the courts. The right of parents and the rights of family take precedence over those of Washington-based bureaucrats and social engineers.

But the fight against parental notification is really only one example of many attempts to water down traditional values and even abrogate the original terms of American democracy. Freedom prospers when religion is vibrant and the rule of law under God is acknowledged. When our Founding Fathers passed the first amendment, they sought to protect churches from government interference. They never intended to con struct a wall of hostility between government and the concept of religious belief itself.

The evidence of this permeates our history and our government. The Declaration of Independence mentions the Supreme Being no less than four times. "In God We Trust" is engraved on our coinage. The Supreme Court opens its proceedings with a religious invocation. And the Members of Congress open their sessions with a prayer. I just happen to believe the schoolchildren of the United States are entitled to the same privileges as Supreme Court Justices and Congressmen.

Last year, I sent the Congress a constitutional amendment to restore prayer to public schools. Already this session, there's growing bipartisan support for the amendment, and I am calling on the Congress to act speedily to pass it and to let our children pray.

Perhaps some of you read recently about the Lubbock school case, where a judge actually ruled that it was unconstitutional for a school district to give equal treatment to religious and nonreligious student groups, even when the group meetings were being held during the students' own time. The first amendment never intended to require government to discriminate against religious speech.

Senators Denton and Hatfield have proposed legislation in the Congress on the whole question of prohibiting discrimination against religious forms of student speech. Such legislation could go far to restore freedom of religious speech for public school students. And I hope the Congress considers these bills quickly. And with your help, I think it's possible we could also get the constitutional amendment through the Congress this year.

More than a decade ago, a Supreme Court decision literally wiped off the books of 50 States statutes protecting the rights of unborn children. Abortion on demand now takes the lives of up to 1 1/2 million unborn children a year. Human life legislation ending this tragedy will some day pass the Congress, and you and I must never rest until it does. Unless and until it can be proven that the unborn child is not a living entity, then its right to life, liberty, and the pursuit of happiness must be protected.

You may remember that when abortion on demand began, many, and, indeed, I'm sure many of you, warned that the practice would lead to a decline in respect for human life, that the philosophical premises used to justify abortion on demand would ultimately be used to justify other attacks on the sacredness of human life—infanticide or mercy killing. Tragically enough, those warnings proved all too true. Only last year a court permitted the death by starvation of a handicapped infant.

I have directed the Health and Human Services Department to make clear to every health care facility in the United States that the Rehabilitation Act of 1973 protects all handicapped persons against discrimination based on handicaps, including infants. And we have taken the further step of requiring that each and every recipient of Federal funds who provides health care services to infants must post and keep posted in a conspicuous place a notice stating that "discriminatory failure to feed and care for handicapped infants in this facility is prohibited by Federal law." It also lists a 24-hour, toll-free number so that nurses and others may report violations in time to save the infant's life.

In addition, recent legislation introduced in the Congress by Representative Henry Hyde of Illinois not only increases restrictions on publicly financed abortions, it also addresses this whole problem of infanticide. I urge the Congress to begin hearings and to adopt legislation that will protect the right of life to all children, including the disabled or handicapped.

Now, I'm sure that you must get discouraged at times, but you've done better than you know, perhaps. There's a great spiritual awakening in America, a renewal of the traditional values that have been the bedrock of America's goodness and greatness.

One recent survey by a Washington-based research council concluded that Americans were far more religious than the people of other nations; 95 percent of those surveyed expressd a belief in God and a huge majority believed the Ten Commandments had real meaning in their lives. And another study has found that an overwhelming majority of Americans disapprove of adultery, teenage sex, pornography, abortion, and hard drugs. And this same study showed a deep reverence for the importance of family ties and religious belief.

I think the items that we've discussed here today must be a key part of the Nation's political agenda. For the first time the Congress is openly and seriously debating and dealing with the prayer and abortion issues—and that's enormous progress right there. I repeat: America is in the midst of a spiritual awakening and a moral renewal. And with your Biblical keynote, I say today, "Yes, let justice roll on like a river, righteousness like a never-failing stream."

Now, obviously, much of this new political and social consensus I've talked about is based on a positive view of American history, one that takes pride in our country's accomplishments and record. But we must never forget that no government schemes are going to perfect man. We know that living in this world means dealing with what philosophers would call the phenomenology of evil or, as theologians would put it, the doctrine of sin.

There is sin and evil in the world, and we're enjoined by Scripture and the Lord Jesus to oppose it with all our might. Our nation, too, has a legacy of evil with which it must deal. The glory of this land has been its capacity for transcending the moral evils of our past. For example, the long struggle of minority citizens for equal rights, once a source of disunity and civil war, is now a point of pride for all Americans. We must never go back. There is no room for racism, anti-Semitism, or other forms of ethnic and racial hatred in this country.

I know that you've been horrified, as have I, by the resurgence of some hate groups preaching bigotry and prejudice. Use the mighty voice of your pulpits and the powerful standing of your churches to denounce and isolate these hate groups in our midst. The commandment given us is clear and simple: "Thou shalt love thy neighbor as thyself."

But whatever sad episodes exist in our past, any objective observer must hold a positive view of American history, a history that has been the story of hopes fulfilled and dreams made into reality. Especially in this century, America has kept alight the torch of freedom, but not just for ourselves but for millions of others around the world.

And this brings me to my final point today. During my first press conference as President, in answer to a direct question, I pointed out that, as good Marxist-Leninists, the Soviet leaders have openly and publicly declared that the only morality they recognize is that which will further their cause, which is world revolution. I think I should point out I was only quoting Lenin, their guiding spirit, who said in 1920 that they repudiate all morality that proceeds from supernatural ideas—that's their name for religion—or ideas that are outside class conceptions. Morality is entirely subordinate to the interests of class war. And everything is moral that is necessary for the annihilation of the old, exploiting social order and for uniting the proletariat.

Well, I think the refusal of many influential people to accept this elementary fact of Soviet doctrine illustrates an historical reluctance to see totalitarian powers for what they are. We saw this phenomenon in the 1930's. We see it too often today.

This doesn't mean we should isolate ourselves and refuse to seek an understanding with them. I intend to do everything I can to persuade them of our peaceful intent, to remind them that it was the West that refused to use its nuclear monopoly in the forties and fifties for territorial gain and which now proposes 50-percent cut in strategic ballistic missiles and the elimination of an entire class of land-based, intermediate-range nuclear missiles.

At the same time, however, they must be made to understand we will never compromise our principles and standards. We will never give away our freedom. We will never abandon our belief in God. And we will never stop searching for a genuine peace. But we can assure none of these things America stands for through the so-called nuclear freeze solutions proposed by some.

The truth is that a freeze now would be a very dangerous fraud, for that is merely the illusion of peace. The reality is that we must find peace through strength.

I would agree to a freeze if only we could freeze the Soviets' global desires. A freeze at current levels of weapons would remove any incentive for the Soviets to negotiate seriously in Geneva and virtually end our chances to achieve the major arms reductions which we have proposed. Instead, they would achieve their objectives through the freeze.

A freeze would reward the Soviet Union for its enormous and unparalleled military buildup. It would prevent the essential and long overdue modernization of United States and allied defenses and would leave our aging forces increasingly vulnerable. And an honest freeze would require extensive prior negotiations on the systems and numbers to be limited and on the measures to ensure effective verification and compliance. And the kind of a freeze that has been suggested would be virtually impossible to verify. Such a major effort would divert us completely from our current negotiations on achieving substantial reductions.

A number of years ago, I heard a young father, a very prominent young man in the entertainment world, addressing a tremendous gathering in California. It was during the time of the cold war, and communism and our own way of life were very much on people's minds. And he was speaking to that subject. And suddenly, though, I heard him saying, "I love my little girls more than anything—" And I said to myself, "Oh, no, don't. You can't —don't say that." But I had underestimated him. He went on: "I would rather see my little girls die now, still believing in God, than have them grow up under communism and one day die no longer believing in God."

There were thousands of young people in that audience. They came to their feet with shouts of joy. They had instantly recognized the profound truth in what he had said, with regard to the physical and the soul and what was truly important.

Yes, let us pray for the salvation of all of those who live in that totalitarian darkness—pray they will discover the joy of knowing God. But until they do, let us be aware that while they preach the supremacy of the state, declare its omnipotence over individual man, and predict its eventual domination of all peoples on the Earth, they are the focus of evil in the modern world.

It was C.S. Lewis who, in his unforgettable "Screwtape Letters," wrote: "The greatest evil is not done now in those sordid 'dens of crime' that Dickens loved to paint. It is not even done in concentration camps and labor camps. In those we see its final result. But it is conceived and ordered (moved, seconded, carried and minuted) in clear, carpeted, warmed, and well-lighted offices, by quiet men wth white collars and cut fingernails and smooth-shaven cheeks who do not need to raise their voice."

Well, because these "quiet men" do not "raise their voices," because they sometimes speak in soothing tones of brotherhood and peace, because, like other dictators before them, they're always making "their final territorial demand," some would have us accept them at their word and accommodate ourselves to their aggressive impulses. But if history teaches anything, it teaches that simple-minded appeasement or wishful thinking about our adversaries is folly. It means the betrayal of our past, the squandering of our freedom.

So, I urge you to speak out against those who would place the United States in a position of military and moral inferiority. You know, I've always believed that old Screwtape reserved his best efforts for those of you in the church. So, in your discussions of the nuclear freeze proposals, I urge you to beware the temptation of pride—the temptation of blithely declaring yourselves above it all and label both sides equally at fault, to ignore the facts of history and the aggressive impulses of an evil empire, to simply call the arms race a giant misunderstanding and thereby remove yourself from the struggle between right and wrong and good and evil.

I ask you to resist the attempts of those who would have you withhold your support for our efforts, this administration's efforts, to keep America strong and free, while we negotiate real and verifiable reductions in the world's nuclear arsenals and one day, with God's help, their total elimination.

While America's military strength is important, let me add here that I've always maintained that the struggle now going on for the world will never be decided by bombs or rockets, by armies or military might. The real crisis we face today is a spiritual one; at root, it is a test of moral will and faith.

Whittaker Chambers, the man whose own religious conversion made him a witness to one of the terrible traumas of our time, the Hiss-Chambers case, wrote that the crisis of the Western World exists to the degree in which the West is indifferent to God, the degree to which it collaborates in communism's attempt to make man stand alone without God. And then he said, for Marxism-Leninism is actually the second oldest faith, first proclaimed in the Garden of Eden with the words of temptation, "Ye shall be as gods."

The Western World can answer this challenge, he

wrote, "but only provided that its faith in God and the freedom He enjoins is as great as Communism's faith in Man."

I believe we shall rise to the challenge. I believe that communism is another sad, bizarre chapter in human history whose last pages even now are being written. I believe this because the source of our strength in the quest for human freedom is not material, but spiritual. And because it knows no limitation, it must terrify and ultimately triumph over those who would enslave their fellow man. For in the words of Isaiah: "He giveth power to the faint; and to them that have no might. He increased strength. . . . But they that wait upon the Lord shall renew their strength; they shall mount up with wings as eagles; they shall run, and not be weary. . . ."

Yes, change your world. One of our Founding Fathers, Thomas Paine, said, "We have it within our power to begin the world over again." We can do it, doing together what no one church could do by itself.

God bless you, and thank you very much.

Yuri Andropov
Statement
September 28, 1983

The Soviet leadership deems it necessary to make
known to Soviet people, other peoples and all those
who are responsible for shaping the policy of states its
assessment of the course pursued in international affairs
by the present U.S. Administration.

Briefly speaking, it is a militarist course which poses
a grave threat to peace. Its essence is to try and assure
for the United States dominant positions in the world
without reckoning with the interests of other states and
peoples.

Precisely these aims are served by the unprecedented
build-up of the U.S. military potential, the large-scale
programmes of manufacturing weapons of all types—
nuclear, chemical and conventional. Now it is planned
to project the unrestricted arms race into outer space as
well.

American military presence thousands of kilometres
from U.S. territory is expanded under spurious pretexts
of all kinds. Bridgeheads are set up for direct armed
interference in the affairs of other states, and for the use
of American weapons against any country which re-
jects Washington's diktat. As a result, tensions have
grown the world over—in Europe, Asia, Africa, the
Middle East and Central America.

Other NATO countries are increasingly being involved in the implementation of these dangerous plans
of Washington. More, efforts are being made to revive

119

Japanese militarism and hitch it to the bloc's military-political machine. In doing so, people are being induced to forget the lessons of the past.

The peoples judge the policy of a government primarily by its actions. That is why when the U.S. President grandiloquently holds forth from the United Nations rostrum about commitment to the cause of peace, self-determination and sovereignty of peoples, these are mere declamatory statements that can convince no one.

If anyone had any illusions about a possible evolution for the better in the policy of the present American Administration, such illusions have been completely dispelled by the latest developments. For the sake of its imperial ambitions, that Administration goes to such lengths that one begins to doubt whether Washington has any brakes at all to prevent it from crossing the line before which any sober-minded person must stop.

The insidious provocation involving a South Korean plane engineered by U.S. special services is also an example of extreme adventurism in politics. We have elucidated thoroughly and authentically the factual aspect of this act. The guilt of its organizers, however they might prevaricate and whatever false versions they might put forward, has been proved.

The Soviet leadership has expressed regret over the loss of human lives due to that unprecedented, criminal subversion. Those lives are on the conscience of those who would like to arrogate to themselves the right not to reckon with the sovereignty of states and the inviolability of their borders, who masterminded and carried out the provocation, who literally on the following day hastily pushed through Congress colossal military appropriations and are now rubbing their hands in glee.

Thus, the "humanism" of the statesmen who are seeking to blame others for the death of the people aboard the plane is materialized in new mountains of weapons of mass destruction—from MX missiles to containers with nerve gas.

In their striving somehow to justify their dangerous, inhuman policies, these same people heap slander on the Soviet Union and on socialism as a social system, with the tone being set by the U.S. President himself. One must say bluntly—the spectacle of the leaders of a country like the United States resorting with the aim of smearing the Soviet people, to what amounts well-nigh to obscenities alternating with pharisaical preachments about morality and humanism is an unattractive sight.

The world knows well the worth of such moralizing. In Vietnam morality, as understood by Washington leaders, was introduced with napalm and toxic agents, in Lebanon it is being hammered in by the salvoes of naval guns, in El Salvador this morality is being imposed by genocide. And the list of crimes could be continued. So we have something to say about the moral aspect of the U.S. policy as well: both by recalling history and speaking about the present time.

Today in Washington, together with morality, elementary norms of decency are being trampled and disrespect shown not only for statesmen and states, but also for the United Nations Organization. The question arises: can the international organization, called upon to maintain peace and security, remain in a country where an outrageous militarist psychosis is being implanted and the good name of the organization besmirched?

Under the cover of anti-communism, the claimants

to the role of arbiters of the destinies of the world are seeking to impose their order wherever they do not encounter a rebuff.

The concepts used to justify such a manner of action would not in themselves merit attention if not for the fact that they are preached by leaders of a major power, and not merely preached, but are carried out in practice.

The transfer of ideological contradictions to the sphere of interstate relations has never benefited those who resorted to it in external affairs. To do so today, in the nuclear age, is simply absurd and inadmissible. To turn the battle of ideas into military confrontation would be too costly for the whole of mankind.

But those who are blinded by anti-communism are evidently incapable of grasping this. Starting with the bogey of a "Soviet military threat," they have now proclaimed a "crusade" against socialism as a social system. Attempts are made to persuade people that in general there is no room for socialism in the world. True, they do not specify that what they mean is the kind of world Washington would wish to see.

But wishes and possibilities are far from being the same thing. It is given to no one to reverse the course of history. The U.S.S.R. and other socialist countries will live and develop according to their own laws—the laws of the most advanced social system.

In the six and a half decades of its existence the Soviet state has successfully withstood many trials, including severe ones. Those who attempted to encroach on the integrity of our state, its independence and our system found themselves on the garbage heap of history. It is high time that everybody to whom this applies understood that we shall be able to ensure the security of our country, the security of our friends and allies under any circumstances.

Soviet people can rest assured that our country's defence capability is maintained at such a level that it would not be advisable for anyone to stage a trial of strength.

For our part, we do not seek such a trial of strength. The very thought of it is alien to us. We do not set the well-being of our people, the security of the Soviet state apart from, let alone counterpose them to the well-being and security of other peoples, other countries. In the nuclear age one should not look at the world through the narrow prism of one's selfish interests. Responsible statesmen have only one choice—to do everything possible to prevent a nuclear catastrophe. Any other position is shortsighted, more, it is suicidal.

The Soviet leadership does not hesitate in deciding what line to follow in international affairs in the present acute situation too. Our course continues to be projected at preserving and strengthening peace, lessening tension, curbing the arms race and expanding and deepening co-operation between states. This is the immutable will of the Communist Party of the Soviet Union, of all Soviet people. These are, we are convinced, also the aspirations of all peoples.

Of course, the malicious attacks on the Soviet Union produce here a natural feeling of indignation, but we have strong nerves, and we do not base our policy on emotions. Our policy rests on common sense, realism, a sense of profound responsibility for the destinies of the world.

We proceed from the premise that mankind is not doomed to destruction. The arms race can and must be terminated. Mankind deserves a better fate than living in a conflict-rent world, suffocating under the burden of deadly weapons.

In advancing far-reaching proposals on limitation and reduction of nuclear armaments, both strategic and medium-range, in Europe, we show our concern not only for the security of the U.S.S.R., the states of the socialist community, but also for the security of all other countries.

As regards U.S. policy, its growing militarization is manifested also in the unwillingness to conduct serious talks of any kind, to reach agreement on questions of curbing the arms race.

The Soviet-American talks on the burning problem—reduction of nuclear armaments in Europe—have been going on for two years now. The position of the Soviet side is directed at finding mutually acceptable solutions on a fair, just basis, solutions which do not infringe anyone's legitimate interests. At the same time, these two years have made it clear that our partners in the talks at Geneva are by no means there to reach an accord. Their task is different—to play for time and then start the deployment in Western Europe of ballistic Pershing 2 and long-range cruise missiles. And they do not particularly try to conceal this.

All they do is prattle about some flexibility of the United States at the Geneva talks. Another portion of such "flexibility" has just materialized. And this time too the inbuilt deception is clear. Leaving details aside, the essence of the so-called new move in the U.S. position, vaunted as "superb," boils down to the proposal to agree, as before, on how many Soviet medium-range missiles should be reduced and how many new American missiles should be deployed in Europe, in addition to the nuclear potential already possessed by NATO.

In short, we are asked to talk about how to help the NATO bloc to upset to its advantage the balance of medium-range nuclear systems in the European zone. And this move is blandly presented as something new.

The operation of stationing these American nuclear missiles in Europe is seen from the Washington control tower as perfectly simple and maximally advantageous for the United States—advantageous at the expense of Europe. The European allies of the U.S. are regarded as hostages. This is a frank, but cynical policy. But what is really unclear is this: do those European political leaders who—disregarding the interests of their peoples, the interests of peace—are helping to implement the ambitious militaristic plans of the U.S. Administration give thought to this?

Here nothing should be left unsaid. If, contrary to the will of the majority of people in West European countries, American nuclear missiles appear in the European continent, this will be a major move fundamentally inimical to peace on the part of the U.S. leaders and the leaders of other NATO countries who act at one with them.

Neither do we see any willingness on the American side to tackle in earnest the problem of limiting and reducing strategic armaments. In the American capital they are busy launching the production of ever new systems of these armaments as well. And on the approaches are types of these weapons that may radically upset the concept of strategic stability and the very possibility of effective limitation and reduction of nuclear arms.

No one should mistake for a sign of weakness the Soviet Union's good will and desire to reach agreement. The Soviet Union will be able to make a proper response to any attempt to disrupt the existing military-strategic balance, and its words and deeds will not be at variance

However, we are in principle opposed to competition in the production and stockpiling of weapons of mass annihilation. This is not our path. It cannot lead to the solution of any of the problems facing mankind, i.e. economic development of states, preservation of the environment, creation of at least elementary conditions for people's life, nourishment, health and education.

Release of the material resources recklessly squandered on the arms race, and the unfolding of man's boundless creative potentialities—this is what can unite people, what should determine the policy of states at the turn of the 20th and 21st centuries. For all this to be realized, the forces of militarism must be checked, and the world be kept through concerted effort from sliding into an abyss.

All peoples, every inhabitant of our planet, should realize the danger that threatens. Realize, in order to join efforts in the struggle for their own survival.

Mankind has not lost, nor can it lose, its reason. This is clearly manifested by the great scope of the anti-missile, anti-war movement which has developed in the European and other continents, a movement in which people of different social, political, and religious affiliation participate.

All who raise today their voice against the senseless arms race and in defence of peace can be sure that the policy of the Soviet Union, of other socialist countries, is directed at attaining precisely these aims. The U.S.S.R. wants to live in peace with all countries, including the United States. It does not nurture aggressive plans, does not impose the arms race on anyone, does not impose its social order on anyone.

Our aspirations and strivings are implemented in concrete proposals directed at effecting a decisive turn for the better in the world situation. The Soviet Union will continue to do everything possible to uphold peace on earth.

Ronald Reagan
Foreign Policy Address
January 16, 1984

During the first days of 1984, I would like to share with you and the people of the world my thoughts on a subject of great importance to the cause of peace—relations between the United States and the Soviet Union.

Tomorrow, the United States will join the Soviet Union and 33 other nations at a European disarmament conference in Stockholm. The conference will search for practical and meaningful ways to increase European security and preserve peace.

We will be in Stockholm with the heartfelt wishes of our people for genuine progress. We live in a time of challenges to peace but also of opportunities to peace.

Through times of difficulty and frustration America's highest aspiration has never wavered. We have and will continue to struggle for a lasting peace that enhances dignity for men and women everywhere.

I believe that 1984 finds the United States in the strongest position in years to establish a constructive and realistic working relationship with the Soviet Union. We've come a long way since the decade of the 70's, years when the United States seemed filled with self-doubt and neglected its defenses while the Soviet Union increased its military might and sought to expand its influence by armed forces and threat.

Over the last 10 years, the Soviets devoted twice as much of their gross national product to military expenditures as the United States, produced six times as many ICBM's, four times as many tanks, twice as many combat aircraft. And they began deploying the SS-20 intermediate-range missile at a time when the United States had no comparable weapon.

History teaches that wars begin when governments believe the price of aggression is cheap. To keep the peace, we and our allies must be strong enough to convince any potential aggressor that war could bring no benefit, only disaster. So, when we neglected our defenses, the risks of serious confrontation grew.

Three years ago, we embraced a mandate from the American people to change course. And we have. With the support of the American people and the Congress, we halted America's decline. Our economy is now in the midst of the best recovery since the 60's. Our defenses are being rebuilt, our alliances are solid and our commitment to defend our values has never been more clear.

America's recovery may have taken Soviet leaders by surprise. They may have counted on us to keep weakening ourselves. They've been saying for years that our demise was inevitable. They said it so often they probably started believing it. Well, if so, I think they can see now they were wrong.

This may be the reason that we've been hearing such strident rhetoric from the Kremlin recently. These harsh words have led some to speak of heightened uncertainty and an increased danger of conflict. This is understandable but profoundly mistaken.

Look beyond the words and one fact stands out. America's deterrence is more credible, and it is making the world a safer place. Safer because now there is less danger that the Soviet leadership will underestimate our strength or question our resolve.

Yes, we are safer now. But to say that our restored deterrence has made the world safer is not to say that it's safe enough. We're witnessing tragic conflicts in many parts of the world. Nuclear arsenals are far too high, and our working relationship with the Soviet Union is not what it must be.

These are conditions which must be addressed and improved. Deterrence is essential to preserve peace and protect our way of life, but deterrence is not the beginning and end of our policy toward the Soviet Union.

We must and will engage the Soviets in a dialogue as serious and constructive as possible, a dialogue that will serve to promote peace in the troubled regions of the world, reduce the level of arms and build a constructive working relationship.

Neither we nor the Soviet Union can wish away the differences between our two societies and our philosophies, but we should always remember that we do have common interests. And the foremost among them is to avoid war and reduce the level of arms.

There is no rational alternative but to steer a course which I would call credible deterrence and peaceful competition. And if we do so, we might find areas in which we could engage in constructive cooperation.

Our strength and vision of progress provide the basis for demonstrating with equal conviction our commitment to stay secure and to find peaceful solutions to problems through negotiations.

That's why 1984 is a year of opportunities for peace. But if the United States and the Soviet Union are to rise to the challenges facing us, seize the opportunities for peace, we must do more to find areas of mutual interest and then build on them.

I propose that our Governments make a major effort to see if we can make progress in three broad problem areas.

First, we need to find ways to reduce and eventually to eliminate the threat and use of force in solving international disputes. The world has witnessed more than 100 major conflicts since the end of World War II. Today there are armed conflicts in the Middle East, Afghanistan, Southeast Asia, Central America and Africa. In other regions, independent nations are confronted by heavily armed neighbors seeking to dominate by threatening attack or subversion.

Most of these conflicts have their origins in local problems, but many have been exploited by the Soviet Union and its surrogates. And of course, Afghanistan has suffered an outright Soviet invasion.

Fueling regional conflicts and exporting violence only exacerbate local tensions, increase suffering and make solutions to real social and economic problems more difficult.

Further, such activity carries with it the risk of larger confrontations. Would it not be better and safer if we could work together to assist people in areas of conflict in finding peaceful solutions to their problems. That should be our mutual goal.

But we must recognize that the gap in American and Soviet perceptions and policy is so great that our immediate objective must be more modest.

As a first step, our Governments should jointly examine concrete actions that we both can take to reduce the risk of U.S.-Soviet confrontation in these areas.

And if we succeed, we should be able to move beyond this immediate objective.

Our second task should be to find ways to reduce the vast stockpiles of armaments in the world. It's tragic to see the world's developing nations spending more than $150 billion a year on armed forces, some 20 percent of their national budgets.

We must find ways to reverse the vicious cycle of threat and response which drives arms races everywhere it occurs.

With regard to nuclear weapons, the simple truth is America's total nuclear stockpile has declined. Today we have far fewer nuclear weapons than we had 20 years ago. And in terms of its total destructive power, our nuclear stockpile is at the lowest level in 25 years.

Just three months ago, we and our allies agreed to withdraw 1,400 nuclear weapons from Western Europe. This comes after the withdrawal of 1,000 nuclear weapons from Europe three years ago. Even if all our planned intermediate-range missiles have to be deployed in Europe over the next five years—and we hope this will not be necessary—we would have eliminated five existing nuclear weapons for each new weapon deployed.

But this is not enough. We must accelerate our efforts to reach agreements that will greatly reduce nuclear arsenals, provide greater stability and build confidence.

Our third task is to establish a better working relationship with each other, one marked by greater cooperation and understanding. Cooperation and understanding are built on deeds, not words. Complying with agreements helps; violating them hurts.

Respecting the rights of individual citizens bolsters the relationship; denying these rights harms it. Expanding contacts across borders and permitting a free exchange or interchange of information and ideas increase confidence; sealing off one's people from the rest of the world reduces it. Peaceful trade helps, while organized theft of industrial secrets certainly hurts.

Cooperation and understanding are especially important to arms control. In recent years, we've had serious concerns about Soviet compliance with agreements and treaties. Compliance is important because we seek truly effective arms control.

However, there's been mounting evidence that provisions of agreements have been violated and that advantage has been taken of ambiguities in our agreements.

In response to a Congressional request, a report on this will be submitted in the next few days. It is clear that we cannot simply assume that agreements negotiated will be fulfilled. We must take the Soviet compliance record into account, both in the development of our defense program and in our approach to arms control.

In our discussions with the Soviet Union, we will work to remove the obstacles which threaten to undermine existing agreements and the broader arms control process.

Examples I've cited illustrate why our relationship with the Soviet Union is not what it should be. We have a long way to go, but we're determined to try and try again. We may have to start in small ways, but start we must.

In working on these tasks, our approach is based on three guiding principles: realism, strength and dialogue.

Realism means we must start with a clear-eyed understanding of the world we live in. We must recognize that we are in a long-term competition with a Government that does not share our notions of individual liberties at home and peaceful change abroad. We must be frank in acknowledging our differences and unafraid to promote our values.

Strength is essential to negotiate successfully and protect our interests. If we're weak, we can do neither. Strength is more than military power. Economic strength is crucial, and America's economy is leading the world into recovery. Equally important is our strength of spirit and unity among our people at home and with our allies abroad.

We're stronger in all these areas than we were three years ago. Our strength is necessary to deter war and to facilitate negotiated solutions. Soviet leaders know it makes sense to compromise only if they can get something in return. But America can now offer something in return.

Strength and dialogue go hand in hand. We're determined to deal with our differences peacefully through negotiations. We're prepared to discuss the problems that divide us and to work for practical, fair solutions on the basis of mutual compromise. We will never retreat from negotiations.

I have openly expressed my view of the Soviet system. I don't know why this should come as a surprise to Soviet leaders who've never shied from expressing their view of our system. But this doesn't mean that we can't deal with each other.

We don't refuse to talk when the Soviets call us imperialist aggressors and worse. Or because they cling to the fantasy of a Communist triumph over democracy. The fact that neither of us likes the other's system is no reason to refuse to talk. Living in this nuclear age makes it imperative that we do talk.

Our commitment to dialogue is firm and unshakeable, but we insist that our negotiations deal with real problems, not atmospherics. In our approach to negotiations, reducing the risk of war, and especially nuclear war, is priority No. 1. A nuclear conflict could well be mankind's last.

And that is why I proposed over two years ago the zero option for intermediate-range missiles. Our aim was and continues to be to eliminate an entire class of nuclear arms. Indeed, I support a zero option for all nuclear arms. As I've said before, my dream is to see the day when nuclear weapons will be banished from the face of the earth.

Last month, the Soviet Defense Minister stated that his country would do everything to avert the threat of war. Well, these are encouraging words, but now is the time to move from words to deeds. The opportunity for progress in arms control exists. The Soviet leaders should take advantage of it.

We have proposed a set of initiatives that would reduce substantially nuclear arsenals and reduce the risk of nuclear confrontation. The world regrets—certainly we do—that the Soviet Union broke off negotiations on intermediate-range nuclear forces and has not set a date for the resumption of the talks on strategic arms and on conventional forces in Europe.

Our negotiators are ready to return to the negotiating table to work toward agreements in I.N.F., Start and M.B.F.R. We will negotiate in good faith. Whenever the Soviet Union is ready to do likewise, we'll meet them halfway.

We seek to reduce nuclear arsenals and to reduce the chances for dangerous misunderstanding and miscalculation. So we have put forward proposals for what we call confidence-building measures. They cover a wide range of activities.

In the Geneva negotiations, we've proposed to exchange advance notifications of missile tests and major military exercises. Following up on Congressional suggestions, we also proposed a number of ways to improve direct channels of communication.

Last week, we had productive discussions with the Soviets here in Washington on improving communications, including the hotline. Now these bilateral proposals will be broadened at the conference in Stockholm. We're working with our allies to develop practical, meaningful ways to reduce the uncertainty and potential for misinterpretation surrounding military activities and to diminish the risk of surprise attack.

Arms control has long been the most visible area of U.S.-Soviet dialogue. But a durable peace also requires ways for both of us to defuse tensions and regional conflicts.

Take the Middle East as an example. Everyone's interest would be served by stability in the region. And our efforts are directed toward that goal. The Soviets could help reduce tensions there instead of introducing sophisticated weapons into the area. This would certainly help us to deal more positively with other aspects of our relationship.

Another major problem in our relationship with the Soviet Union is human rights. Soviet practices in this area, as much as any other issue, have created the mistrust and ill will that hangs over our relationship.

Moral considerations alone compel us to express our

deep concern over prisoners of conscience in the Soviet Union and over the virtual halt in the emigration of Jews, Armenians and others who wish to join their families abroad.

Our request is simple and straight-forward: that the Soviet Union live up to its obligations. It has freely assumed those obligations under international convenants, in particular, its commitments under the Helsinki accords. Experience has shown that greater respect for human rights can contribute to progress in other areas of the Soviet-American relationship.

Conflicts of interest between the United States and the Soviet Union are real, but we can and must keep the peace between our two nations and make it a better and more peaceful world for all mankind.

Our policy toward the Soviet Union, a policy of credible deterrence, peaceful competition and constructive cooperation, will serve our two nations and people everywhere. It is a policy not just for this year but for the long term. It's a challenge for Americans; it is also a challenge for the Soviets.

If they cannot meet us halfway, we will be prepared to protect our interests and those of our friends and allies. But we want more than deterence. We seek genuine cooperation. We seek progress for peace.

Cooperation begins with communication. As I've said, we'll stay at the negotiating tables in Geneva and Vienna.

Furthermore, Secretary Shultz will be meeting this week with Soviet Foreign Minister Gromyko in Stockholm. This meeting should be followed by others, so that high-level consulations become a regular and normal component of U.S.-Soviet relations.

Our challenge is peaceful. It will bring out the best

in us. It also calls for the best in the Soviet Union. We do not threaten the Soviet Union. Freedom poses no threat; it is the language of progress.

We proved this 35 years ago, when we had a monopoly on nuclear weapons and could have tried to dominate the world, but we didn't. Instead, we used our power to write a new chapter in the history of mankind.

We helped rebuild war-ravaged economies in Europe and the Far East, including those of nations who had been our enemies. Indeed, those former enemies are now among our staunchest friends.

We can't predict how the Soviet leaders will respond to our challenge. But the people of our two countries share with all mankind the dream of eliminating the risk of nuclear war. It's not an impossible dream, because eliminating these risks is so clearly a vital interest for all of us.

Our two countries have never fought each other. There's no reason why we ever should. Indeed, we fought common enemies in World War II. Today, our common enemies are poverty, disease and, above all, war.

More than 20 years ago. President Kennedy defined an approach that is as valid today as when he announced it. "So let us not be blind to our differences," he said, "but let us also direct attention to our common interests and to the means by which those differences can be resolved."

Well, those differences are differences in Government structure and philosophy. The common interests have to do with the things of everyday life for people everywhere.

Just suppose with me for a moment that an Ivan and

an Anya could find themselves, oh, say, in a waiting room or sharing a shelter from the rain or a storm with a Jim and Sally. And there was no language barrier to keep them from getting acquainted.

Would they then debate the differences between their respective Governments? Or would they find themselves comparing notes about their children and what each other did for a living? Before they parted company, they would probably have touched on ambitions and hobbies and what they wanted for the children and problems of making ends meet.

And as they went their separate ways, maybe Anya would be saying to Ivan: "Wasn't she nice. She also teaches music." And Jim would be telling Sally what Ivan did or didn't like about his boss. They might even have decided they were all going to get together for dinner some evening soon.

Above all they would have proven that people don't make wars. People want to raise their children in a world without fear and without war. They want to have some of the good things over and above bare subsistence that make life worth living. They want to work at some craft, trade or profession that gives them satisfaction and a sense of worth. Their common interests cross all borders.

If the Soviet Government wants peace, then there will be peace. Together we can strengthen peace, reduce the level of arms and know in doing so that we have helped fulfill the hopes and dreams of those we represent and, indeed, of people everywhere.

Let us begin now.

ABOUT THE AUTHOR

STROBE TALBOTT is the diplomatic correspondent of *Time* Magazine. He is the translator-editor of *Khrushchev Remembers* and *Khrushchev Remembers: The Last Testament* (Little, Brown, 1970 and 1974), the author of *Endgame: The Inside Story of SALT II* (Harper & Row, 1979), and *Deadly Gambits,* a history of the START and INF negotiations to be published later this year by Alfred A. Knopf, Inc. He is also a contributor to two Council on Foreign Relations books: *The China Factor,* published with the American Assembly, 1981, and *The Making of America's Soviet Policy,* to be published this spring by Yale University Press.